MIDDLESEX COUNTY, VIRGINIA

DEED BOOK ABSTRACTS

1709-1720

Ruth and Sam Sparacio

The Antient Press Collection
from

Colonial Roots
Millsboro, Delaware
2016

Colonial
Roots

Helping You Grow Your Family Tree

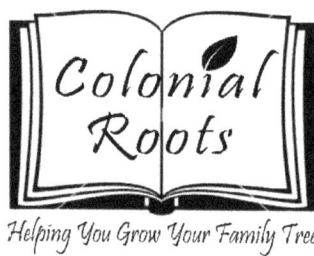

ISBN 978-1-68034-106-5

CONTENTS

[this page intentionally blank]

p. 220   KNOW ALL MEN by these presents that we HANNAH PROVERT, CHARLES LEE and HENRY GOODLOE of Middlesex County are bound unto MATTHEW KEMP Gent. first in Commission of peace for said County in sume of Three hundred pounds Sterl. this 6th day of March 1709.

The Condition of this obligation is such that if Hanah Provert Administr. of the Estate of WILLIAM PROVERT deced do make a true inventory of said Deced Estate and do exhibit the same to ye next Court and make oath thereto and truely administer the sd Estate according to Law that then this obligation to be voyd otherwise to remain

In presence of WIL. STANARD   Hanah Probert

Chas. Lee   Henry Goodloe

Acknowledged in open Court held for Middlesex County the 6th day of March 1709 by the Subscribers to it and admitted to record

pp. 220-221   KNOW ALL MEN by these presents that we JANE MEACHAM, JAMES MEACHAM, JOHN ALLDIN & ROBERT NORMAN are bound unto JOHN SMITH Gentl. first in Commission of peace for Middlesex County in sume of five hundred and fifty pounds Sterl. money of England this 2d day of January 1709.

The Condition of this obligation is such that whereas Administration of the Estate of JOSEPH MEACHAM deced is by the Justices granted to Jane Meacham Now if said Jane Meacham shall return a perfect inventory to the next Court and shall render a true account of said Estate when required by the Court and keep the Justices from troubles about the said Estate that then this obligation to be voyd or else to stand

In presence of HARRY BEVERLEY,   Jane Meacham

WIL. STANARD   James Meacham, John Alldin

Robert Norman

Acknowledged in Court held for Middlesex County the 2d day of January 1709 by the Subscribers to it and admitted to record

p. 221   KNOW ALL MEN by these presents that wee JOHN MERCY and RICE CURTIS are bound unto MATHEW KEMP Gent first in Comission of the peace for County of Middlesex in sume of one hundred pounds Sterl. this 6th day of March 1709.

The Condition of this obligation is such that if the above bound John Mercy Administrator of the Estate of JOHN YARRANTON deced do make a true inventory of all the goods chattles and creditts of said deced and do truely administer ye said Estate according to Law and shall pay unto such persons as the Court shall appoint then this obligation to be voyd otherwise to remain in force

In presence of WM. JONES,   Jno. M Mercy

Rice Curtis

Acknowledged in Court held for Middlesex County the 6th day of March 1709 and admitted to record

pp. 221-222   KNOW ALL MEN by these presents that we WILLIAM GORDON, HARRY BEVERLEY and JOHN VIVION of Middlesex County are bound unto MATTHEW KEMP Gent first in Comission of peace for said County in sume of one hundred pounds Sterl. this 6th day of March 1709.

The Condition of this obligation is such that if William Gordon Administrator of the Estate of RICHD. GABRIELL deced do make a perfect inventory and Exhibit the same at next

Court and make oath and give a true account of his Administration when required that
then this obligation to be voyd otherwise to remain
In presence of WM. DARE,   Wm. Gordon
      WIL. STANARD   Harry Beverley   Jno. Vivion
   Acknowledged in Court held for Middlesex County the 6th day of March 1709 and admitted to record

p.   KNOW ALL MEN by these presents that wee ROBERT LOGAN, WILLIAM GORDON
222   and JNO. HIPKINGS of County of Middlesex are bound unto our Sovereign Lady
       Anne in the sume of Ten thousand pounds of good sweet scented Tobacco & Caske
this 6th day of March 1709.
   The Condition of this obligation is such that Whereas Robert Logan hath obtained a
Lycence to keep an ORDINARY at his house in this County if said Robert Logan doth find
in his said Ordinary good and cleanly lodgeing and Dyatt for travellers and stableage
provender and fodder or pasturage for their horses as the seasons require the terme of
one whole year from ye date hereof and not permitt unlawfull gameing nor on the
Sabbath day suffer any to tipple more than is necessary that then this obligation to be
voyd otherwise to remaine
In presence of us JNO. CURTIS,   Robert Logan
      WIL. STANARD   Wm. Gordon   Jno. Hipkings
   Acknowledged in Court held for Middlesex County the 6th day of March 1709 and admitted to record

p.   KNOW ALL MEN by these presents that wee GEORGE CHOWNING, THOMAS CHOW-
222   NING and EDMUND MICKLEBURROUGH of County of Middlesex are bound unto
       MATTHEW KEMP Gent first in Comission of Peace for said County in sume of one
hundred pounds Sterling this 3d day of Aprill 1710.
   The Condtion of this obligation is such that if George Chowning do truely pay unto
JOHN CHOWNING Orphan of ROBERT CHOWNING deced all estate as soon as he the said
orphan shall attaine to lawfull age and keep harmless the Justices from said Estate that
then this obligation to be voyd otherwise to remain
                              George Chowning
                     Thomas Chowning   E. Mickleburrough
   Acknowledged in Court held for Middlesex County the 3d day of Aprill 1710 and admitted to record

p.   KNOW ALL MEN by these presents that we RICHARD KEMP, GEORGE WORTHAM
223   and JOHN SMITH Gent. are bound to our Sovereign Lady the Queen in the sume of
       one thousand pounds Sterl. money of England this first day of May 1710.
   The Condition of this obligation is such that Whereas Richard Kemp is by the Honble
the Presidents Commission dated the 27th day of Aprill 1710 appointed Sheriff of the
abovesaid County of Middlesex Now if said Richard Kemp shall render unto Mr. Auditor
DIGGS a full account of all Revenues in said County and due payment make of all pub-
lick dues leveyed and true performance make of Office of Sheriff that then the above
obligation to be voyd or else to remaine
In presence of WIL. STANARD,   Richard Kemp
      JNO. CURTIS   George Wortham   John Smith
   At a Court held for Middlesex County the 1st day of May 1710
This bond was acknowledged by the subscribers to it and admitted to record

p.   KNOW ALL MEN by these presents that we JOHN OWEN, MINOR MINOR and RICE
223   CURTIS of Middlesex County are bound unto MATTHEW KEMP Gent first in Comis-
       sion of the peace for said County in sume of one hundred pounds Sterl. this first
day of May 1710.

 The Condition of this obligiation is such that if John Owen do truely pay to ALEXANDER
MAHOLLAND all such Estate due to ye said Orphan as soon as he shall attaine to lawfull
age and keep the Justices from all trouble about the Estate that then the above obligation to be voyd otherwise to remaine

In presence of WILLIAM BARBEE,   John Owen
     WILLIAM STANARD   Minor Minor   Rice Curtis

  Acknowledged in Court held for Middlesex County the first day of May 1710 by the subscribers to it and admitted to record

pp.   KNOW ALL MEN by these presents that we WILLIAM CHURCHHILL Esqr. and
223-   WILLIAM STANARD of Middlesex County are bound unto MATTHEW KEMP Gent
224   first in the Comission for said County in sum of fifty pounds Sterl. this first day
       of May 1710.

 The Condition of this obligiation is such that if William Churchhill Esqr. Administrator
of the Estate of JAMES BASKIT deced do make a perfect inventory of all the goods of the
said deced and exhibit the same to next Court and make a true account of his said Ad-
ministracon when lawfully called then this obligation to be voyd otherwise to remaine

                                            W. Churchhill
                                            Wil. Stanard

  Acknowledged in Court held for Middlesex County the first day of May 1710 by the Subscribers to it and admitted to record

p.   KNOW ALL MEN by these presents that I WILLIAM FALKNER of the County of
224   Middx. Planter have sold unto JNO. CLARKE of County of GLOSTER Carpenter four
       cows and three heifers and five steers marked with a cropp and underkeel and
one fether bed & one Seelskin trunk and ovel table and two keetells six ould chaires for
consideration of twenty pounds Sterl. and do warrant the sale of said goods Witness my
hand this 4th day of June 1709.

Test   AVERILLA HARDEE   Wm. Falkner

 At a Court held for Middlesex County the 5th day of June 1710
The above was proved by the Oath of Averilla Hardee and admitted to record

p.   KNOW ALL MEN by these presents that We JOSEPH HUTCHINSON and MARY his
224   Wife and THEOPHILUS MAN of Middlesex County are bound unto MATTHEW KEMP
       Gent first in Comission of ye peace for said County in sum of two hundred
pounds Sterling money this 5th day of June 1710.

 The Condition of this obligation is such that if Joseph Hutchinson Adminitr: of the Estate of DOROTHY NEEDLES deced do make a true Inventory of said Estate and exhibit ye
same to ye next Court and truely administer said Estate according to law and payment
make as the Court shall appoint that then this obligacon to be voyd otherwise to remain

In presence of JNO. CURTIS,   Joseph ♃ Hutchinson
     WIL. STANARD   Theophilus Man

  At a Court held for Middx. County the 5th day of June 1710
This bond was acknowledged by the subscribers to it and admitted to record

p.
225
SURVEYED and Divided the 27th day of Aprill 1710 for and between FRANCIS CHOWNING, GEORGE CHOWNING, MATTHEW CRANK, JOHN CHOWNING and WILLIAM CHOWNING three hundred and Eighty acres of land (thirty six acres whereof purchased by ROBERT CHOWNING Father of ye aforesaid Chownings being included) the said land lying on both sides of the MAINE ROAD in Middlesex County and divided and by lotts appointed by consent of all persons as following To each lott Seventy six acres of land John & William Chowning being under age consenting by their guardians to Thomas Chowning the lott towards Rappahanock River at ye lowest end of said land; to John Chowning lott lying on boths sides afsd Road at ye lower end of land; to George Cowning the lott next above Thomas and Johns lotts; to Matthew Crank and his Wife the lott next above George Chowining; to William Chowning the upper most lott. The Lotts being bounded as the severall platts bearing date with these presents and given to them under the hand of HARRY BEVERLEY Surveyor.
At a Court held for Middlesex County the 5th of June 1710
This Division of the land among the Orphans of Robert Chowning deced was presented in Court by Thomas Chowning and Matthew Crank who marryed one of ye deced Daughters and admitted to record.

pp.
225-
226
THIS INDENTURE made the twentieth & fourth day of May 1710 Between RICHARD DANIELL of County of Middlesex of one part and JOHN SMITH and JAMES SMITH of same County Witnesseth that sd Richard Daniell for sum of Five pounds ten shillings Sterling money hath sold unto said John Smith and James Smith their heirs forever Eight acres and a halfe of land in County of Middlesex being part of One hundred and fifteen acres of land sold to WILLIAM DANIELL by CUTHBERT POTTER by Deed of Sale dated March 17th 1669 and now belonging unto said Richard Daniell the said Eight acres and a halfe of land being bounded begining on the East side of the Mill Dam belonging to the said John and James Smith at a marked white oake so runing East along the line that parteth the said land and land of ALEXANDER SMITH to a marked red oake sappling and from thence West South West to the Mill Branch that part of said land and the land of ALEXANDER MURRY and up the said Mill Dam to the first beginning
In presents of us JNO. VIVION,   Richard Daniell
    JOHN KEIGHLEY, ELIZA. X SMITH,   John Smith   James Smith
    JOHN ϑ CLARKE
At a Court held for Middlesex County the 5th day of June 1710
Richard Daniell came into Court and acknowledged his Deed to Capt. John Smith and Mr. James Smith which is admitted to record

p.
226
KNOW ALL MEN by these presents that wee WILLIAM KILPIN, HARRY BEVERLEY & JOHN ROBINSON of County of Middlesex are bound unto our Sovereign Lady Anne in the sum of ten thousand pounds of Tobacco & caske this 3d July 1710
The Condition of this obligation is such that Whereas William Kilpin hath obtained a Lycence to keep an ORDINARY at his house in this County in the BURGH of URBANNA if therefore said William Kilpin doth provide wholesome lodgeing and dyett for travellers and stableage provinder and fodder or pasturage as the seasons require for their horses dureing terme of one whole year from day of date hereof and not permitt unlawfull gameing nor on the Sabbath day suffer any to tipple more than is necessary that then this oblgiation to be voyd otherwise to be in full force
                                    W. Kilpin
                        Harry Beverley Jno. Robinson
Acknowledged in Court held for Middlesex County the 3d day of July 1710 by the Subscribers to it and admitted to record

pp.   BY THIS PUBLICK INSTRUMENT or Letter of Attorney be it known that on the
226-   thirtieth day of October 1709 and in the Eighth year of the Reign of our Sove-
227   reign Lady Anne & before ROBERT FORRENS Notary Publick dwelling in London
        and in presence of witnesses personally appeared Mr. ROBERT WISE of London
Merchant which appearer hath made Messrs. JOHN PRATT & NATHANL. BURWELL of
Yorke River in Virginia Merchants to be my full attornys giveing full power to demand
and sue for of any person in Virginia such sums of money, goods and things whatsoever are oweing unto said Constituent and generally to accomplish what the Constituant could do if present
In presence of BARTHO: HOSKINS,   Robert Wise
    SAML. SMITH, JOSIAH THOMAS Robt. Forrens Not. Pub.
  At a Court held for Middlesex County the 3d day of July 1710
This Letter of Attorney proved in Court by the Oath of Bartholomew Hoskins and
admitted to record

p.   KNOW ALL MEN by these presents that wee ROBERT CARTER, GEORGE BEVERICK
227   WILLIAM CHURCHHILL and WM. STANARD are bound unto GAWIN CORBIN Gent
        first in the Comission of the peace for County of Middlesex in sum of two hun-
dred and sixty nine pounds & Six shillings and Nine pence this 3d day of July 1710
   The Condition of this obligation is such that Whereas upon an action of Trespass upon
the Case brought in Middlesex County Court against said George Beverick by said Gawin
Corbin who hath at Court for said County on the third day of July 1710 recovered Judgment against the said George Beverick for one hundred and thirty four pounds fourteen shillings and Two pence and Whereas the said George Beverick hath prayed an
appeal from the Judgment to ye Lt. Governour and Councill on the 8th day of next
Generall Court Now if said George Beverick shall present the said appeal and if he be
cast in said suit and satisfy the judgement of said Generall Court that then this obligation to be voyd otherwise to stand
                              Robert Carter
                    W. Churchhill   Wil. Stanard
   At a Court held for Middx. County the 3d day of July 1710
This bond was acknowledged by the Subscribersd to it and admitted to record

pp.   Virginia SS KNOW ALL MEN by these presents that I JOHN NEEDLES of the Pro-
227-   vince of MARYLAND gent do appoint my loveing friends Collo (blurred) and my
228   loveing Brother in Law Mr. THOMAS STAPLETON of Middlesex County in Virginia
        to receive of all persons money or Tobo: due to me and appoynt my said Attor-
neys to defend all manner of persons that shall lay clayme to any part of my land lately
sold to RICHARD STEEVENS ratifying my said attorneys whatsoever shall lawfully do In
Witness whereof I have set my hand and Seal this 5th day of October 1703
In presence of us R. STEEVENS,   John Needles
    JOHN SANDIFORD, RICHARD SHELFORD
   At a Court held for Middlesex County the 3d day of July 1710
This Letter of Attorney was this day proved in Court by Oath of John Sandiford and
admitted to record

p.   1710 THOMAS STAPLETON & EDMUND HAMERTON Administratrs: of Estate of JOHN
228   STAPLETON charging themselves with all the Estate as Followeth Vizt. To Sundry
        goods and chattles as pr Inventory and appraisement returned in Court Total
3336 Tobo.; to WILLIAM BARBEEs Neat; to JOSEPH HUTCHINSONs do; to THEOPHILUS STAN-
TON do; and the said Adminrs. pay allowance for the following debts of the said Estate as

followeth EDMD. HAMERTON by THOMAS STAPLETON By Sheriff By GEOR. CLAY Judgt. in Court Cr 3464

At a Court held for Middlesex County the 3d day of July 1710
Produced in Court by Thomas Stapleton & Edmd. Hamerton ye Administrs. and at their motion admitted to record

p. Middlesex County Sct WHEREAS severall laws have appointed Fifty acres of land
228 for a TOWN and whereas We CHRISTOPHER ROBINSON, HARRY BEVERLEY and
JOHN ROBINSON by Order of Middlesex County Court dated the 4th of June 1704 appointed Feoffees in Trust to make sale of said land KNOW ALL MEN therefore that we Feoffees as aforesaid for sume of One hundred and fifty five pounds of Tobacco and Caske paid by SAML. BROWN have sold one lott of land in the BURGH of URBANNA containing Eleven pole one way and Eight ye other makeing one long square being bounded on the North by QUEENS STREET on the West by EAST LANE and on East by a Lott of land sold to Mr. WILLIAM GORDON To Hold as is directed by Act of Assembly October 1705 paying one ounce of Flax seed and two ounces of Hemp seed on the tenth of October annually to the Director and Benchers of said Burgh of Urbanna provided that said Saml. Brown shall cause to be built one good house to containe twenty foot square within Twelve months. In Witness we have set our hands and seales this 17th day of September 1706
In presence of JOHN SMITH,   Chr. Robinson
JNO. VIVION   Jno. Robinson
At a Court held for Middlesex County the 7th day of August 1710
Harry Beverley and John Robinson Gent. came into Court and acknowledged this their Deed to the heires of SAML. BROWN deced which is admitted to record

p. Middlesex County Sct WHEREAS severall Laws have appointed fifty acres of land
229 for a TOWN and Whereas CHRISTOPHER ROBINSON, HARRY BEVERLEY and JOHN
ROBINSON by Order of Middlesex County Court the 4th day of June 1704 appointed Feoffees in Trust to make sale of the said land Know All Men that we Feoffees as aforesaid for sume of one hundred and fifty pounds of Tobacco and caske do sell unto SAMLL. BROWN one halfe acres in the BURGH of URBANNA lying opposite to EAST LANE on North side of QUEEN STREET To Hold as is directed by Act of Assembly at Williamsburgh the 23d day of October 1705 paying rent of one ounce of Flax seed and two ounces of Hemp seed on the tenth of October annually to the Director or Benchers of the said Burgh of Urbanna provided that said Samuell Brown shall within twelve months build a house on said lott in Witness whereof we have set our hands and seales this 17th day of September 1706
In presence of us JOHN SMITH   Chrs. Robinson
JNO. VIVION   Jno. Robinson   Harry Beverley
At a Court held for Middx. County the 7th day of August 1710
Harry Beverley and John Robinson came into Court and acknowledged this Deed to the heires of Mr. Saml. Brown deced which is admitted to record

p. Middx. County Sct WHEREAS severall laws have appointed fifty acres of land for
229 a TOWN and whereas we CHRISTOPER ROBINSON, HARRY BEVERLEY and JOHN
ROBINSON are appointed Feoffess in Trust to make sale of the said land KNOW ALL MEN that we the said Feoffees in Trust for sume of one hundred and Sixty five pounds of Tobacco and caske have sold unto WILLIAM GORDON one lott of land in the BURGH of URBANNA Eleven poles one way and eight the other lying on the South side of QUEEN STREET the first lott upon the Creek To Hold as directed by Genl. Assembly the 23d day of

October 1705 paying annually one ounce of Flax seed and two ounces of Hemp seed on
the tenth day of October to the Director and Benchers of said Burgh of Urbanna pro-
vided said Wm. Gordon within twelve months build one good house In Witness whereof
we have set our hands and seals this 17th day of September 1706
In presence of JOHN SMITH,   Chrs. Robinson
    JNO. VIVION   Harry Beverley Jno. Robinson
  At a Court held for Middx. County the 7th day of August 1710
Harry Beverley and John Robinson Gent came into Court and acknowledged this Deed to
William Gordon which is admitted to record

p.   Middx. County Sct. WHEREAS severall laws have appointed fifty acres of land for
230   a TOWN and Whereas we CHRISTOPHER ROBINSON, HARRY BEVERLEY and JOHN
      ROBINSON are appointed Feoffees in Trust to make sale of said land KNOW ALL
MEN that we the said Feoffees for the sume of one hundred and eighty seven pounds of
Tobacco have sold unto Mr. WILLIAM GORDON and his heirs one halfe acre of land in
the BURGH of URBANNA lying on the East side of EAST LANE and faceing QUEEN STREET
and so down to the Creek on the South side by two Lotts taken up by him the said
William Gordon To Hold as is directed by Act of the Genl. Assembly dated the 23d day of
October 1705 paying annually one ounce of Flax seed and two ounces of Hemp seed on
the tenth day of October to the Director or Benchers of said Burgh of Urbanna provided
said William Gordon shall begin on said lott within twelve months one good house In
Witness whereof we have set our hands and Seales this Ninth day of June 1707
In presence of JOHN SMITH,   Chrs. Robinson
    JNO. VIVION   Jno. Robinson   Harry Beverley
  At a Court held for Middx. County the 7th day of August 1710
Harry Beverley and John Robinson acknowledged this Deed to Mr. William Gordon
which is admitted to record.

pp.   Middx. County Sct WHEREAS severall laws have appointed fifty acres of land for
230- a TOWN and Whereas we CHRISTOPHER ROBINSON, HARRY BEVERELY and JOHN
231   ROBINSON are appointed Feoffees in Trust to make sale of said land KNOW ALL
     MEN that said Feoffees for the sume of one hundred and eighty pounds of Tobac-
co and caske have sold one lott of land unto Mr. WILLIAM GORDON on QUEEN STREET on
the North side and on West side of the lott taken up by Mr. SAMUEL BROWN To Hold
paying annually one ounce of Flax seed and two ounces of Hemp seed to the Director
and Benchers of the Burgh of Urbanna provided that William Gordon within twelve
months build one good house In Witness whereof we have set our hands and seales this
9th day of June 1707
In presence of JNO. SMITH,   Chr. Robinson
    JOHN VIVION   Jno. Robinson   Harry Beverley
  At a Court held for Middx. County the 7th day of August 1710
Harry Beverley and John Robinson acknowledged this Deed to Mr. William Gordon
which is admitted to record

p.   Middlesex County Sct WHEREAS severall laws have appointed to Middlesex
231   County land for a TOWN and Whereas CHRISTOPHER ROBINSON, HARRY BEVERLEY
     and JOHN ROBINSON are appointed Feoffees in Trust to sell said lands NOW this
Indenture that said Feoffess as aforesaid for sume of three hundred and seventy four
pounds of Tobacco and caske paid by Mr. WILLIAM GORDON have sold two lotts of land in
the BURGH of URBANNA on the North side of QUEENS STREET on the West side of CROSS
LANE To Hold paying annually one ounce of Flax seed and two ounces of Hemp seed to

the Director and Benchers provided he build one good house within twelve months In Witness whereof we have set our hands and seales this 17th day of March 1708
In presence of ANNE ANDERSON,   Harry Beverley
    ELIZABETH BEVERLEY   Jno. Robinson   Christopher Robinson
  At a Court held for Middx. County the 7th day of August 1710
Harry Beverley and John Robinson acknowledged their Deed to Mr. William Gordon
which is admitted to record

pp.   Middlesex County Sct WHEREAS severall laws have appointed Fifty acres of land
231- for a TOWN and Whereas CHRISTOPHER ROBINSON, HARRY BEVERLEY and JOHN
232   ROBINSON are appointed Feoffees in Trust to sell the said land NOW this Inden-
     ture that said Feoffees in Trust for the sume of one hundred and fifty pounds of
Tobacco and Caske do sell unto Mr. WILLIAM GORDON one lott of land in the BURGH of
URBANNA being on the North side of QUEENS STREET the first lott upon the Creek To
Hold paying annually one ounce of Flax seed and two ounces of Hemp seed to the Director and Benchers of said Burgh of Urbanna provided that within twelve months he
build one good house In Witness whereof we have set our hands and seales this 17th day
of September 1706
In presence of JOHN SMITH,   Harry Beverley
    JNO. VIVION   Jno. Robinson   Christopher Robinson
  At a Court held for Middx. County the 7th day of August 1710
Harry Beverley and John Robinson acknowledged their Deed to Mr. William Gordon
which is admitted to record

pp. Seal of   WHEREAS her Majesty out of her Royall grace to her Subjects
233- Colony   hath been pleased to signify to me her royall Will for preserving
234   unto them their Legall rights and properties which said Instruc-
     tions are as followeth WHEREAS we are above all things desireous that all our
Subjects may enjoy their legall rights and properties you are to take speciall care that
if any person be committed for any criminall matter (unless for Treason or felony
plaintly and especially expressed in the warrant of Committment) he have free liberty
to petition by himselfe or otherwise the Cheife Baron or any one of the Judges of ye
Comon Pleas for a Writt habeas Corpus which upon such application shall be granted
and served on the Provost Marshall Goaler or other Officers having the Custody of such
persons or shall be left at the goal or place where the prisoner is consined and the said
Provost Marshall or other officer shall within three days after such service (on the
Petitioner paying the fees and charges and giveing Security that he will not Escape by
the way) make return of the said Writt and prisoner before the Judge who granted out
the said Writt and there Certifie the true cause of the imprisonment and the said Barron
or Judge shall discharge such prisoner takeing his recognizance and surety for his ap-
pearance at the Court where the offence is cognizable and certify the said Writt and
recognizance into ye Court unless such offences appear to the Barron or Judge not
baileable by Law of England and in case the said Baron or Judge shall refuse to grant a
Writt of habeas Corpus in view of the Copy of Committment or upon oath made of such
copy haveing been denyed the prisoner or any person requiring the same on . . . . his
behalfe or deny to discharge the prisoner after the granting of such Writt the said
Barron or Judge shall incurr the forfeiture of his place. You are likewise to declare our
pleasure that in case the Provost Marshall or other officer shall imprison any person
above twelve hours Except by a mittimus setting forth the cause thereof he be removed
from his said office. And upon the application of any person wrongfully committed the
Barron or Judge shall issue his Warrant to the Provost Marshall or other Officer to

bring ye prisoner before him who shall be discharged without baile or paying fees and the Provost Marshall or other officer refusing Order to such Warrant shall be there-upon removed and if said Barron or Judge Denies his Warrant he shall likewise incurr the forfeiture of his place. You shall give directions that no prisoner cast at Large by an habeas Corpus be recommitted for the same offence but by the Court where he is bound to appear and if any Barron, Judge, Provost Marshall or other officer contrary hereunto shall recommend such persons so bailed or delivered you are to remove him from his place and if the Provost Marshall or other officer haveing the custody of the Prisoner neglects to return the habeus Corpus or refuses a copy of the Comitment within six hours after demand made by the prisoner or by others in his behalfe shall Likewise incurr the forefeiture of his place and for the better prevention of long im-prisonments you are to appoint two Courts of Oyer and Terminer to be held yearly Vizt. on the second Tuesday in December and the second Tuesday in June the charge whereof to be paid by the public & treasurey of our said Colony not Exceeding L 100 each Session You are to take care that all prisoners in case of Treason or Felony have the Liberty of petition in open Court for their tryall that they be Indicted at the first Court of Oyer and Terminer unless it appears upon Oath that the Witnesses against them could not be pro-duced and that they be tryed the second Court or discharged And the Barron or Judge upon the motion made the last day of the Sessions in open Court is to baile the prisoner or upon the refuseall of the sd Barron or Judge and Provost Marshall or other Officers to do their respective dutys herein they shall be removed from their place, provided always that no person be discharged out of prison who stands committed for Debt for any Decree of Chancery or any legall proceedings of any Court of record and for the preventing of any Exactions that may be incure upon the Prisoner, you are to declare our pleasure that no barron or Judge shall receive for himself or Clerks for Granting a Writt of habeas Corpus more than two shillings six pence and the lyke sum for takeing a recognizance and that the Provost Marshall shall not receive more than Five shil-lings for every Committment One shilling three pence for the bond the prisoner is to signe One shilling three pence for a copy of a Mittimus and one shilling and three pence for Every mile he bringeth back ye prisoner. In Obedience to her Majty Comands and to the intent that all her Subjects may be fully inform'd how much they owe to her Majtys royall Favour for these her gracious Concession I ALEXANDER SPOTS-WOOD Esqr. her Majts. Lt. Governor of her Colony and Dominion of Virginia have thought fit by and with the advice of her Majts. Councill to issue this my Proclamation hereby comanding in her Majts. name the Sheriffs of the respective Countys within this Colony to cause this Signification of her Majties pleasure to be openly read and published at the respective Court houses of their respective Countys at ye next Court after the receipt hereof and I do further with the advice aforesaid require and comand the Justices of the respective County Court to cause the same to be registred in the records of the sd Countys and to observe these her Majties comands as they will answer to the Contrary at their perrill. Given at WmBurgh under my hand wth the seale of the Colony this 6th day of July 1710 in the Ninth year of her Majty. Reign

   GOD SAVE THE QUEEN   A. Spotswood

At a Court held for Middx. County the 7th day of August 1710
This Proclamation was this day published in Court and admitted to record

p. At a Councill held at the Capitoll lthe 5th day of July 1710
234 Present The Honoble; Lieutennant Governor in Councill - ORDERED that all and
    every person and persons haveing any office within this Governmt. whereby
any fees do accrew to him do transmitt to the Honble. the Lieut. Governor by the fourth day of the next Generall Court a fair table of the fees by them charged for each pticular

Service done in their said Offices and cause like fair tables of their fees to be hung up
in their sd Offices and they are hereby strictly Enjoyned not to exact from any of her
Majties Subjects any other or greater fees then what are mentioned in said Table
To be published at Court for her Majty Service   WIL. ROBERTSON Cl Con
To the Sheriff of the County of Middx.
    At a Court held for Middx. County the 7th day of August 1710
This order of Councill was this day read in Court and admitted to record

p.   KNOW ALL MEN by these presents that we WILLIAM YOUNG, EDMUND HAMERTON
235   and ALEXANDER GRAVES are bound unto MATTHEW KEMP Gent First in Comis-
          sion of the peace for Middlesex County in sum of one hundred pounds Sterl.
money of England this 7th day of August 1710.
    The Condition of this obligation is such that Whereas administration of the Estate of
THOMAS MORRIS deced is by Court granted unto William Young by order of Court Now if
said Wm. Young shall returne a true inventory of the said Estate to the next Court and
render a true account of all the Estate of the said deced and shall account the same then
this obligation to be voyd or else to stand
In presence of ZACH. LEWIS,   Wm. Young
                                          Edmd. Hamerton   Alexr: Graves
    At a Court held for Middx. County the 7th day of August 1710
This Bond was presented in Court and acknowledged by the Subscribers to it and admitted to record

pp.   THIS INDENTURE made this 28th day of January 1708/9 Between GEORGE CHOW-
235-   NING of LANCASTER COUNTY of one part and CHARLES COOPER and MARY his
236   Wife of County of Middlesex Witnesseth that said George Chowning for good
          causes especially moveing hath leased to farme lett unto said Charles Cooper
dureing his naturall life and to his said Wife dureing her Widdowhood if she shall happen to survive him a certain parcell of land belonging to sd George Chowning in Middx.
County upon the head of Sunderland Creek bounded beginning at a read oake standing
in JOHN NASHes line on a hill side by an old PATHWAY over a branch a little North from
the path thence over said Branch up a small valley and across said Chownings Old Feild
Easterly to a marked Poplar tree standing by a Rowling Path thence down the said path
to the Rock Hole thence up South West to a corner tree of said branch by the Marsh
thence Northwest to the beginning place To Hold all the land contained within the
bounds aforementioned unto said Charles Cooper dureing his naturall life and to his
Wife as long as she shall remain a Widdow if she survives as aforesaid paying every
year all the Quitrents of said Chownings whole divident of land dureing the said term
and doth aggree with said Charles Cooper that he will make use of as much timber as
will serve to build him a reasonable dwelling house and a forty foot tobacco house
In presence of JOHN NASH,   George Chowning
      JAMES Ɨ BROWN, THOMAS CHOWNING   Charles X Cooper   Mary X Cooper
    At a Court held for Middx. County the 4th day of September 1710
George Chowning came into Court and acknowedged the above Lease to Charles Cooper
and Mary his Wife which is admitted to record

pp.   THIS INDENTURE made this fifth and sixth day of February 1710 Between RICE
236-   JONES of Southfarnham Parish in County of ESSEX of one part and MATTHEW COX
237   of Parish & County aforesaid Witnesseth that for sume of three thousand pounds
          of Tobacco and caske paid to said Rice Jones he doth sell unto said Mathew Cox
his heirs in his actuall possession by Vrtue of bargain & Sale made (and by virture of

Statute for transferring uses into possession) tract of land in County of Middlesex at the upper end of the said County (being part of a Devident of land belonging to said Rice Jones bounding on the Draggon Swamp) containing Fifty acres of land bounded begin- ning at a Poplar standing in the mouth of a small branch thence running up a line of marked trees thence Northeast to a Stake being a corner of said Jones's land thence South West to the place it began

In presence of G. CORBIN,   Rice Jones
    ZACHARY LEWIS, J. HARDEE
    At a Court held for Middlesex County the 6th day of February 1710
Rice Jones came into Court and acknowledged this Lease and Release unto Matthew Cox which is admitted to record.

p.   KNOW ALL MEN by these presents that I JOHN WYATT JUNR. of KING & QUEEN
238   County in Virginia am bound unto GAWIN CORBIN of Middlesex County in the
       penall sum of three hundred and twenty pounds Sterl. this first day of February
1710. The Condition of this obligation is such that if John Wyatt Junr. do hereafter make an Indefeazable Estate of Inheritance in the Law to Gawin Corbin in all that Divi- dent of land in Middlesex County bounded on the Dragon Swamp formerly the land of RICE JONES deced by Deeds and Evidences sufficient and also if the same be hereafter continued unto said Gawin Corbin & kept harmless from all manner of other bargains and sales that then this obligation to be voyd or remain effectual

In presence of JOHN CLARKE,   Jno. Wyatt junr.
    THO. HICKMAN JUNR., WILLIAM ℋ JONES
    JACOB ℋℙ PRESNALL
    At a Court held for Middlesex County the 6th day of February 1710
The within bond was proved in Court by the oathes of John Clarke and William Jones which is hereby certified
    At a Court held for Middlesex County the 6th day of March 1710
The within bond was proved by the Oath of Jacob Presnall & admitted to record

p.   THIS INDENTURE made the first day of February 1710 Between JOHN WYATT JUNR
239   of KING and QUEEN COUNTY Son and Heire of ANNE WYATT Daughter of RICE
       JONES late of Middx. County deced of one part and GAWIN CORBIN of County of
Middx. Witnesseth that said John Wyatt for sum of one hundred and sixty pounds Sterl. sold unto said Gawin Corbin his heires all that land whereon JOHN JONES Son of the said Rice Jones deced now liveth on the Dragon Swamp in the County of Middlesex given by the last Will and Testament of said Rice Jones to the said Anne his Daughter and also all by the said Johns Right of remainder and inheritance to the whole of the said tract of land said to containe thirteen hundred acres of land

In presence of us JOHN CLARKE,   Jno. Wyatt junr.
    EDMD. HAMERTON, THO. HICKMAN JUNR.,
    JACOB ℋℙ PRESNALL, WILLIAM ℋ JONES
    At a Court held for Middx. County the 6th day of February 1710
This Deed was proved by the Oaths of John Clarke and William Jones two of the witnesses to it which is hereby Certifyed
    At a Court held for Middx. County the 6th day of March 1710
This Deed was further proved by the oath of Jacob Presnall and admitted to record

pp.   THIS INDENTURE made the first day of May 1711 Between WILLIAM BROOKES of
240-   County of Middlesex Planter of one part and ROBERT DANIELL of the same County
242   Gentl. Witnesseth that said William Brookes for sume of three thousand pounds

of Tobacco doth sell unto said Robert Daniell a parcell of land in said County of Middlesex containing fifty acres of land bounded begining at a Corner hickory of said William Brookes and Robert Daniells land and runing thence West to a marked stump thence South East to the first beginning place being part of three hundred acres of land formerly granted to ROBERT CHOWNING Deced by Patent the 16th day of June 1662 which said Fifty acres of land was lately in the occupation of sd William Brookes but now in the actuall possession of Robert Daniel

In presence of GARRITT MINOR,   Wm. ⊕ Brookes
      JOHN OWENS, ROBERT DANIEL JUNR.

   At a Court held for Middlesex County the 1st day of May 1711
William Brookes came into Court and acknowledged this Deed unto Capt. Robert Daniell which is admitted to record ELIZABETH also the Wife of said William Brookes came into Court and being first examined freely relinquished her right of Dower to the land conveyed which is hereby certifyed

   KNOW ALL MEN by these presents that I William Brookes am bound unto Robert Daniell in the sum of Six thousand pounds of Merchantable Sweet scented Tobacco and caske this first day of May 1711.

   The Condition of this obligation is such that if William Brookes truely observe all covenants mentioned in Indenture of Bargain and Sale that then this obligiation to be voyd otherwise to remain

In presence of GARRETT MINOR,   Wm. ⊕ Brookes
      JOHN OWENS, ROBERT DANIELL JUNR.

   At a Court held for Middlesex County the first day of May 1711
William Brookes acknowledged this bond which is admitted to record

pp. 242-243   KNOW ALL MEN by these presents that I WALTER COCKE of SURREY COUNTY in Virginia Marriner have ordained in my place my trusty and loveing friend Collo. GAWIN CORBIN of County of Middlesex Gent my lawfull Attorney to demand and receive all such sums owing to me from any person whatsoever in Rappahannock or Potomack Rivers in Virginia giving my said Attorney my full authority to perform as fully as I could doe if I was personally present. In Witness whereof I have set my hand and seale the fourth of October 1710.

In presence of EDMD. HAMERTON,   Walter Cocke
      PEN: ♀♀ PERRIOTT (her marke)

   At a Court held for Middlesex County the 6th day of February 1710
This letter of Attorney was proved in Court by the oath of Pen: Perrott which is hereby Certifyed & is admitted to record

p. 243   KNOW ALL MEN by these presents that wee ELIZABETH BEGGARLY, JOHN OWEN and JACOB PRESSENER are bound unto MATTHEW KEMP Gent First in Commission of the peace for Middlesex County in sume of one hundred pounds Sterl. money of England this 6th day of March 1710.

   The Condition of this obligation is such that Whereas Administration of the Estate of CHARLES BEGGARLY deced is by the Court granted unto said Elizabeth as by Order of said County Court Now if said Elizabeth shall returne a perfect inventory of said deced Estate to next Court and render a true account and make just payments to whom of right it shall belong and lawfully administer upon said Estate that then this obligation to be voyd or else to stand

In presence of THOMAS HENENAN,   Elizabeth E Beggarly
      JOHN CURTIS   John Owen   Jacob JP Pressener

At a Court held for Middlesex County the 6th day of March 1710
This bond was acknowledged by the Subscribers to it and admitted to record

p.   KNOW ALL MEN by these presents that we THOMAS ELLIOTT and WILLIAM TIG-
244   NALL are bound unto MATTHEW KEMP Gent First in commission of the peace for
        County of Middlesex in sume of two hundred pounds Sterl. this 5th day of March
1710. The Condition of this obligation is such that if Thomas Elliott shall truely pay unto
WILLIAM DUDLEY and MARY DUDLEY Orphans of JAMES DUDLEY deced all estate as shall
be due to said Orphans as soon as they attain to lawfull age and keep harmless the Justices from trouble about the said Estate that then the above obligation to be voyd otherwise to remaine
In presence of JOHN OWEN,   Thomas Elliott
        WIL. STANARD   William W Tignall
    At a Court held for Middlesex County the 6th day of March 1710
This bond was acknowledged in Court by the subscribers to it and admitted to record

pp.   KNOW ALL MEN by these presents that wee EDWARD CLARKE, GEORGE WORTHAM
244-   and JOHN SMITH gent are bound unto MATTHEW KEMP Gent First in Comission of
245   the peace for County of Middlesex in sume of five hundred pounds Sterl. this 7th
        day of March 1710
The Condition of the above obligation is such that if Edward Clarke truely pay unto
JOHN FERNE Orphan of JOHN FERNE deced all Estate as now and hereafter due as soon as
he shall attain to lawfull age and keep harmless the Justices from trouble concerning
the said Estate that then the above obligation to be voyd otherwise to remain
In presence of ZACHARY LEWIS,   Edward E Clarke
        WIL. STANARD   George Wortham   John Smith
    At a Court held for Middlesex County the 6th day of March 1710
This bond was acknowledged by the subscribers to it and admitted to record

p.   KNOW ALL MEN by these presents that wee JOHN MEACHAM and JOHN BRISTOWE
245   are bound unto MATTHEW KEMP Gent first in commission of the peace for Mid-
        dlesex County in sum of two hundred pounds Sterl. money of England this 6th
day of March 1710
The Condition of this obligation is such that Whereas Admin. of JOHN BRIMs Estate
deced is by the Court granted unto John Meacham and MARY his Wife by order of Court
Now if said John and Mary shall returne a true inventory of said deced Estate to next
Court and render a true account of all the Estate and due payment make to whom of
right it shall belong that then this obligation to be voyd or else to stand
In presence of JOHN OWEN,   John J Meacham
        WIL. STANARD   John Bristow
    At a Court held for Middlesex County the 6th day of March 1710
This bond was acknowledged by the subscribers to it and admitted to record

p.   KNOW ALL MEN by these presents that we THOMAS HASLEWOOD and WILLIAM
246   STANARD are bound unto MATTHEW KEMP Gent first in Commission of the peace
        for Middlesex County in sum of Twenty pounds sterling money of England this
3d day of April 1711.
    The Condition of this obligation is such that Whereas Adminstr. of the Estate of HENRY
GOODRICH deced is by the Court granted unto Thomas Haslewood Now if said Thomas
shall return a true inventory at next Court render a true account of all the estate and
due payments make unto whom of right it shall belong that then this obligation to be

voyd or else to stand
In presence of ROBT. BROOKING,   Tho: ✕ Haslewood
    WM. W GARDNER   Wil. Stanard
  Acknowledged in Court the 3d day of April 1711 by the Subscribers to it and admitted to record.

pp.   KNOW ALL MEN by these presents that wee MARY SHELTON, RICHD. EDWARDS
246- of GLOSTER COUNTY and THOMAS MACHEN are bound unto MATTHEW KEMP gent
247   first in commission of the peace in Middlesex County in sum of Five hundred
      pounds Sterl. money of England this 3d day of Aprill 1711.
  The Condition of this obligation is such that Whereas Adminstr. of the Estate of THO-
MAS SHELTON deced is by the Court granted unto Mary Shelton Now if said Mary Shelton
shall return a true inventory at the next Court and render a true account of all the
Estate and due payments make unto whom of right it shall belong that then this obliga-
tion to be voyd or else to stand
In presence of HARRY BEVERLEY,   Mary Chilton
    WIL. STANARD   Richard Edwards Tho: Machen
  Acknowledged in Court by the Subscribers to it and admitted to record the 3d day of
April 1711.

pp.   THIS INDENTURE made the 28th day of February 1710 Between WILLIAM BAKER
247- SENR. of County of Middlesex of one part and JOSEPH ORPHIN Carpinder of said
248   County Witnesseth that said William Baker hath put as an apprentice to said
      Joseph Orphin his Sonne WILLIAM BAKER dureing the time till he shall come to
      ye age of twenty one years to learn the trade of a Carpinder said apprintice shall
serve his Master his secrets keep lawfull commands obey not committ fornication nor
contract matrimony within the said time att cards dice or any other unlawfull game he
shall not play nor absent himself day nor night from his Masters service without leave
he shall follow any worke and imployment his Master shall put him about except
makeing a Crop of Tobacco and said Joseph Orphin shall cause to be taught or instructed
the said apprintice in trade of a Virga. house carpinder to build Tobacco houses and
common wooden dwelling houses to give Wm. Baker two years schooling to learne to
Reade and cause him to frequent the Church when able to and to provide for him sufficient meate drink apparrell lodging & washing fitting for an apprintice
In presence of MARTHA ✕ HILLARD,   William Baker
    ANNE CONNER   Joseph ✝ Orphin
  Memo that William Baker and Joseph Orphin came this day signed & sealed this Inden-
ture and sd Wm. Baker avers his said Sonn Wm. Baker Junr. to be Eight yeares old the
16th day of December 1710. This done before me the day and year above written
               MATT KEMP one of ye CWC
  At a Court held for Middx. County the 3d day of Aprill 1711
This Indenture was presented in Court by Joseph Orphin and admitted to record

p.   KNOW ALL MEN by these presents that wee RICHARD KEMP, GEORGE WORTHAM
248   and JOHN SMITH of County of Middlesex are bound unto our Sovereign Lady the
      Queen in sume of Forty five thousand one hundred & sixty six pounds of good
sweet scented Tobacco and caske this 3d day of Aprill 1711.
  The Condition of this obligation is such that if Richard Kemp Sheriff shall collect the
Publick & County levies and faithfully pay all said Leavies unto the respective Creditors
for whom they are raised and directed to be paid by Act of Assembly at Generall Assembly at Queen Annes Royall Capitoll the 23d day of October 1705 that then this obligation

to be voyd or else to stand
In presence of HARRY BEVERLEY,   Richd. Kemp
    WIL. STANARD   George Wortham
  Acknowledged in Court the 3d day of April 1711 by the Subscribers to it and admitted to
record

pp.   KNOW ALL MEN by these presents that wee JACOB STIFFE, EDWARD CLARKE and
248- JAMES MEACHAM of the County of Middx. are bound unto Sr. WILLIAM SKIP-
249   WITH Barrontt. first in Comission of the peace for said County in the sum of
        three hundred pounds Sterl. money of England this 3d day of Aprill 1711.
  The Condition of this obligation is such that Whereas Administration upon the Estate of
THOMAS STIFF deced with the Will annexed is granted unto above Jacob as by order of
County Court Now if said Jacob Stiffe shall administer upon the said Estate according to
law and due payments make of said Estate to whom of right it shall belong and at all
times keep the Justices from troubles about the said deceds Estate that then this obliga-
tion to be voyd or else to stand
In presence of WILL YOUNG,   Jacob Stiffe
                  Edward E Clarke   James Meacham
  Acknowledged in Court by the Subscribers and admitted to record ye 3d day of Aprill
1711.

p.   URBANA May the 1st 1711. I doo hereby Impower you Mr. WILLIAM JONES of
249 County of KING and QUEEN Attorney at Law to appear for me at Middx. Court to
     confess judgment to be granted to THOMAS HACKET for one lb eight S Sterling
upon an action brought against me to the aforesaid Court for which shall be your
Warrant
To Mr. William Jones   JAMES STEVENSON
  Admitted to record by Order of Court dated 2 May 1711
  URBANA May the 1st 1711 I doe hereby impower you Mr. WILLIAM JONES of County of
King & Queen Attorney at Law to appear for me at Middx. County Court to confess Judg-
ment to be granted to Mr. WILLIAM KILPIN for 19 lb 10 s. Starling upon an action
brought against me to the aforesaid Court for which this shall be your warrant
To Mr. William Jones   JAMES STEVENSON
  Admitted to record by Order of Court dated 2d day of May 1711
  URBANA May the 1st 1711 I the Subscriber hereof doo hereby Impower Mr. William
Jones of County of King & Queen Attorney att Law to appear for me in all actions that I
am concerned in Middx. County Court and what he shall act I do hereby ratifie Witness
my hand this first day of May 1711,
Test W. KILPIN, JA: WALKER   JAMES STEVENSON
  Recorded

p.   KNOW ALL MEN by these presents that I JAMES BLAISE of County of Middlesex am
250 bound unto WILLIAM MOUNTAGUE of said County in sume of Sixty two pounds
     Sterling money of England this 28th day of March 1699.
  The Condition of this obligation is such that whereas James Blaise in consideration of a
Marriage between himselfe and ELIZA. COCKE suddenly intended to be solemnized doth
promise to pay unto PETER MINOR the Son of the said Eliza. Cocke the sume of thirty one
pounds Sterling money of England when he the said Peter Minor shall attaine to age of
twenty one years and if said James Blaise shall truely pay unto said Peter Minor so soon
as he shall attaine to the ge of twenty one years that this obligation to be voyd or else to
stand always provided that if said Peter Minor shall dye before he attaines the said age

of twenty one years that then this obligation to be voyd and of none effect
In presence of THOMAS STEEL,   .   JAMES BLAISE
          GARRITT MINOR
     At a Court held for Middlesex County the 5th day of June 1711
This bond proved in Court by the oaths of the Witnesses & admitted to record

pp.   KNOW ALL MEN by these presents that I GARRITT MINOR of the County of Mid-
250-   dlesex am bound unto WM. MOUNTAGUE and Mr. TOBIAS MICKLEBURROUGH in the
251   sum of Sixty three pounds seaven shillings and six pence Sterling money of
          England it being part of ye Estate of PETER MINOR left him by his Father DUDIS
MINOR decest I bind myself this 11th day of October 1700.
     The Condition of this obligation is such that Whereas Garit Minor doth oblidge himself
to pay unto Peter Minor the son of Dudis Minor Decest the sum of thirty one pounds
fifteen shiillings and nine pence Sterling money of England so soon as he shall attain
to the age of twenty one years that then this obligation to be voyd or else to stand
In presence of CHRISTOPHER BERNARD,   Garritt Minor
          WM. MOUNTAGUE JUNR.
     At a Court held for Middx. County the 5th day of June 1711
This bond was acknowledged by Garritt Minor the subscriber and admitted to record

pp.   TO ALL CHRISTIAN PEOPLE to whom these presents shall come Wee VALLENTINE
251-   MAYO and ANNE my Wife of County of Middlesex for consideration of the natural
252   affection we bare unto our well beloved Cuzen JONATHAN BROOKS of the afore-
          said County and also for other good causes have granted unto said Jonathan
Brookes and his heires thirty nine acres of land in the County of Middlesex bounded
beginning at a Red oak Corner tree of land of THOMAS OBRISIELS deced and runing West
along an old line of the land of JOHN STAMPER deced to a corner white oak of said
Stampers and HENRY TUGWELL thence North to a Beach by the run of a Swamp called
Mickleburroughs Swamp jest above the HORSE BRIDG thence down and along the said
Swamp to land granted by Pattent to JOHN BOURK deced to a white oak to land of sade
Thomas Obrissle deced and lastly West along the sade Obrissles land to the place it begun
at the sade land being granted by Patent to the sade Vallentine Mayo in the year 1702
In Witness whereof sade Vallintine Mayo and Anne his Wife hath set their hands and
seales this 4th day of June 1711
In presence of JOHN LEWIS,   Vallantine Mayo
          HENRY H BALL, JON. X BONE   Anne A Mayo
     At a Court held for Middlesex County the 5th day of June 1711
Valentine Mayo came into Court and acknowledged the within Deed which is admitted to
record ANNE MAYO also the Wife of said Vallentine appeared in Court and being first
examined freely relinquished her right of Dower which is hereby certified

p.   KNOW ALL MEN by these presents that wee OLIVER SEGAR, GEORGE WORTHAM &
253   GARRITT MINOR Gent of County of Middlesex are bound unto our Sovereign Lady
          the Queen in sum of one thousand pounds Sterl. this fifth day of June 1711.
     The Condition of this obligation is such that Whereas Oliver Segar Gent is by Commis-
sion from the Honble. Lieut. Governour appointed Sheriff of abovesaid County for this
ensueing year if said Oliver Segar Sheriff shall att all time render unto ye auditor a
particular account of all her Majts. Revenues in said County and also due payment make
of all publick & County dues and that he inquire the true quantity of land held in
aforesaid County and returne a perfect list or rentroll of same to her Majts. Auditor and
full performance make of all things pertaining to the office of Sheriff then this obli-

gation to be voyd or else to stand

In presence of us JNO. CURTIS,   Oliver Segar
                   WIL. STANARD   George Wortham   Garritt Minor

At a Court held for Middlesex County the 5th day of June 1711
This bond was acknowledged by the Subscribers to it and admitted to record

pp.   Virginia SS By her Majts. Lt. Governor & Commander in Chief of this Dominion
254-   WHEREAS I have received Complaints of great delays in the administration of
255   Justice through the County Court neglecting to meet on the days appointed for
         holding the same and the Justices refuseing upon frivilous pretences to sitt
when mett for the dispatch of business before them whereby her Majts. Subjects are
frequently obliged to a tedious expensive attendance before they can obtain a determination of their suits and for as much as I am desirous to be informed from whose fault
such delays doe proceed and that I might be the better enabled to distinguish such persons as out of a due regard to the Service of their Country doe regularly attend the administration of Justices in their County Courts -- I have therefore thought fitt by and
with the advice of the Councill to require the Sheriffs of the respective Countys and
they are hereby required that when ever it shall hereafter happen that the Justices
shall neglect to meet on the days appointed for holding their respective Courts or being
meet shall not duely sitt and dispatch the business then depending that he forthwith
Certifie the same to me together with the names of such of the said Justices as were
then present and were hindred from performing their Duty for want of Sufficient
number and I doe further require the said Justices at their next Succeeding Court to
examine into the reasons of the absence of the other Justices or their refusall to act if
mett and to report the same to me by the first opportunity, and that I may be constantly
informed of the proceedings of said County Courts in the speedy administration of Justice I doe hereby require & comand that the Justices of said Courts forthwith transmit to
me and see at every Generall Court from time to time a list of all such causes on their
Docquett as have been depending above the space of Six months the time of their Entry
& continuance and the reason of their being soe long and undetermined -- And Whereas her Majesty hath been graciously pleased to direct that for the more speedy prosecu-
tion of Criminals two Courts of Oyer & Terminer be held yearly on the second Tuesday in
June and the second Tuesday in December I doe hereby publish and make known that
the said Court will be held at the Capitoll on the said respective days and the Justices of
the County Courts and Sheriffs of the Severall Countys are hereby required to observe
and follow the like orders and directions in conveying Criminals to the said Court and
for the Summoning Witnesses and returning the examinations as are appointed by Law
to be observed upon Tryalls of Criminalls at the Generall Court -- And Forasmuch as it
hath been represented to mee that the Under Sheriffs not being sworn to their
Accounts of the Quitrents received by them gives great opportunity to the said Undersheriffs to defraud Her Majesty in the Receipt of the said Revenues I doe hereby Order
the Justices of the respective County Court to cause the Undersheriffs of said County at
Courts held in the Month of March yearly to exhibit upon Oath a Just and true account
of all the Quit Rents received by them and to make oath that the same doth contain a
compleat & true Rent Roll of all the lands they have been able to discover which oaths
shall be Certified by the Clerk of the Court on the foot of the said Rent Rolls and produced by the High Sheriff to the Auditor before he be admitted to pass his Accounts and
that the Sheriffs may be the better informed of their Dutys in the premises I doe hereby order that these presents be entred in the Records of the Respective County Courts
and that the Clerke deliver a Copy thereof to each Sheriff at his entrance upon his
office. Given under my hand and seale of the Colony at Williamsburgh this 23d day of

Aprill 1711 in the Tenth year of her Majts. Reign

　　　　　　　　　　　　　　　　　　A.SPOTSWOOD

A Precept for the due holding of Courts for Conveying
Criminals and for returning Rent rolls .
　At a Court held for Middx. County the 5th day of June 1711
The above Precept was this day published in Court and admitted to record

pp.　　THIS INDENTURE made the third day of July 1711 Between WM. GARDINER of
255-　Christ Church Parish in County of Middlesex Carpenter of one part and MAR-
257　GRATE SYMONDS Widow and WILLIAM SYMONDS Son and heir of WILLIAM SY-
　　　MONDS of Parish and County aforesaid Witnesseth that he the said William Gardiner for sume of three thousand two hundred and twenty five pounds of Merchantable
Tobacco paid to him by ye said William Symonds deced hath sold unto said Margrate Symonds and William Symonds and heirs of said William Symonds a certain Plantation and
Tract of land containing Sixty acres purchased by the said William Gardiner of JOHN
WEST by Deed dated the sixth day of September 1703 and by assignment on the back of
said Deed assigned by said William Gardiner to said William Symond (but was not ack-
nowledged to said Symonds and Recorded in Court as it ought to have been) the said land
& Plantation being now in occupation of said Margrate Symonds
In presence of GEO: STAPLETON,　　　　　　　　　　William W Gardiner
　　　　JOHN CLARKE, JNO. CURTIS
　At a Court held for Middlesex County the 3d day of July 1711
William Gardiner came into Court and acknowledged this Deed which is admitted to
record.

pp.　　THIS INDENTURE QUADRUPARTITITE made the Eighteenth day of August 1709 and
257　in the Eighth year of the Reign of our Lady Anne Between HENRY WOOD Esqr.
265　(Son and Heire of Sir EDWARD WOOD late of the Parish of St. James Westminster
　　　in County of Middlesex in Kingdom of England Knt. deceased and Dame CLARAH
his Wife) and ANNA Wife of the said Henry Wood of the first part and the said Dame
Clara Wood Relict and Administratrix of all the Rights of Sr. Edward Wood of the Second
part EDWIN THACKER and JOHN THACKER sons of EDWIN THACKER late of Middlesex
County in Virginia deceased of the third part and HENRY THACKER, CHICHELEY CORBIN
THACKER and WILLIAM STANARD who (together with the said Edwin Thacker party to
these presents are Executors named in the Last Will and Testament of said Edwin
Thacker deceased bearing date the Second day of Aprill 1704) of the fourth part.
　WHEREAS by Indenture the first day of May 1701 between WILLIAM CHURCHHILL of
Middlesex County in Virginia Gentleman Attorney of said Henry Wood (by the name of
Henry Wood of London Esqr.) Son and heire of said Sir Edward Wood (by the name of Sir
Edward Wood late of the City of Westminster in Kingdom of England deceased) of one
part and said Edwin Thacker deceased of other part the said William Churchhill in name
of Henry Wood by virtue of a Power of Attorney dated the 11th October 1700 in consideration of the sume of five hundred pounds Sterling money of England sold unto said
Edwin Thacker deceased Fourteen hundred and forty two acres of land in County of
Middlesex (that is to say) one tract of land known by name of POTTERS OLD PLANTATION
TRACT containing Four hundred and forty two acres of land and also one other known
by the name of POTTERS QUARTER TRACT containing one thousand acres of land according to the bounds of the first originall Patents which said land formerly belonged
unto CUTHBERT POTTER deceased and by him conveyed to Sir Edward Wood by Deed dated
the 11th June 1687 and acknowledged in Middlesex County Court 4th July 1687 To Hold
unto the said Edwin Thacker deceased his heires and assigns forever and Whereas the

said EDWIN THACKER dyed before any further assurances were made NOW THIS IN-
DENTURE WITNESSETH that for sum of five hundred pounds Sterling three hundred
pounds Sterling whereof by said Edwin Thacker deceased in his life time to said HENRY
WOOD paid and the remaining Two hundred pounds thereof the said Henry Wood by
HENRY THACKER, CHICKELEY CORBIN THACKER and WILLIAM STANARD (three of the
Executors of the said Edwin Thacker deceased) by the hands of ARTHUR BAILEY of
Milend in County of Middlesex in England Esquire) and five shillings a piece of like
money to said Henry Wood and DAME CLARA WOOD by said Edwin Thacker and John
Thacker receipts of which sums they do by these presents acknowledge and discharge
the said Edwin Thacker, John Thacker, Henry Thacker, Chicheley Corbin Thacker and
William Stanard Executors of said Edwin Thacker deceased have sold all that Fourteen
hundred and forty two acres of land and said Henry Wood and ANNE his Wife and Dame
Clara Wood for themselves doth appoint and impower EDWIN CONWAY of ( ) in County of
LANCASTER in Virginia, WILLIAM DAINGERFIELD of County of ESSEX in Virginia and
THOMAS HICKMAN JUNIOR and HENRY HICKMAN of the County of KING and QUEEN in
Virginia aforesaid or any one of them to appear in Middlesex County Court in Virginia
or the Generall Court when requested to acknowledge this to be their severall acts and
deeds

Signed by Henry Wood and Dame Clara Wood   Henry Wood
in presence of us RI: BURBIDGE, GEORGE BEVERICK,   Clara Wood   Anne Wood
        BENJA. GRAVES, GEO. ALLEN,
        RICHARD LEE, SAMUEL PITT
Signed by Ann Wood in presence of
        JOHN MARSDEN, WILLIAM WALKER, WILLIAM DANELSON,
        RICHD.RHHODGSKINSON, WM. M BOMBER
Feb 13 1709 Recd of Henry Thacker, Chicheley Corbin Thacker and William Stanard by
the hands of Arthur Baileley Esqr. Two hundred pounds it being the remaining con-
sideration within mentioned I say received
Witness BENJA. GRAVES,   Henry Wood
        RICHARD LEE, WILLIAM DAWKINS
   At a Court held for Middlesex County the 5th day of June 1711
Benjamin Graves and Richard Lee Gent made oath that they saw Henry Wood Esqr. sign
the Receipt as his act and deed which is hereby Certifyed
   CHARLES CITY COUNTY Sct Att a Court held att Westopher August the third 1710
The Within written Deed from Henry Wood, Clara Wood and Anne Wood to Henry
Thacker, Chicheley Corbin Thacker and William Stanard was proved by the Oath of Capt.
RICHARD BURBIDGE to be Henry Wood and Clara Wood act and deed and that he see them
two sign seal and deliver the Deed as their act and deed and that he see George Beverick,
Benjamin Graves, Richard Lee and Samuell Pitt put their hands to the same as witness
the said Deed and thereupon ordered to be recorded and the same is truely recorded
                         Test LITTLEBURY EPES ClCur
   CHARLES CITY COUNTY SS Att a Court helden at Westopher August third 1710
The Within Written Deed from Henry Wood, Clara Wood and Anne Wood to Henry
Thacker, Chicheley Corbin Thacker and William Stanard was proved to be the act and
deed of Henry Wood and Clara Wood by the oath of GEORGE ALLIN one of the witnesses
thereto and ordered to be recorded and the same is truely recorded
                         Test LITTLEBURY EPES ClCur
   At a Court held for LANCASTER COUNTY the Ninth day of May 1711
Present her Majties Justices JOHN MARSDEN and WILLIAM WALCKER made Oath that the
within Deed is the act and deed of Anne Wood and Richard Lee alsoe made oath the same

is the act and deed of Henry Wood and Dame Clara Wood
                                   Test JO: TAYLOE
Att a Court held for Middlesex County the fifth day of June 1711
The within Deed was proved in Court to be the act and deed of Henry Wood Esqr. and
Dame Clara Wood to the Executors of Edwin Thacker deced by the oaths of Benjamin
Graves and Richard Lee Gent two of the witnesses thereto which is hereby certified
                                   Wil. Stanard ClCur
At a Court held for ESSEX COUNTY the 14th day of June 1711
WILLIAM BOMBER one of the Witnesses do hereby make oath that he saw Anne Wood
one of the parties to this Deed sign and seal the same as her act and deed
                                   Test RICHARD BUCKNER ClCur
At a Court held for Middlesex County the third day of July 1711
Henry Hickman one of the Attorneys in the above Deed mentioned came this day into
Court and acknowledged the above Deeds to be the severall acts and deeds of Henry Wood
Esqr. Dame Clara Wood and Mrs. Anne Wood to the Executors of Edwin Thacker deced
which Deeds together with the severall proofes and endorsements at motion of said
Executors on behalf of Edwin and John Thacker Sons of said Edwin Thacker deceased are
admitted to record.

pp.   THIS INDENTURE made this Second day and Third day of July 1711 Between
265-   POWELL STAMPER of County of Middlesex County Planter of one part and JOHN
268   LEWIS of same County Planter Whereas said Powell Stamper by Indenture dated
        the day before this date hath sold unto said John Lewis land in the County of
Middlesex and bounded beginning at a Spanish oake corner tree of RICHARD LEWIS
deced or a red oak of Mr. EDWIN THACKER deced thence North to a Black Oake along a
double marked line to a red oak Corner tree of PATRICK MANION and VALENTINE MAYO
thence Southerly to a red oak of Valentine Mayo or THOMAS OBRISLE deced thence
along the line of Edwin Thacker deced to the beginning place To Hold unto the said
John Lewis the terme of one year to the intent that by virtue of the Statute for Transferring uses into possession said Powell Stamper to grant and release unto said John
Lewis Now This Indenture Witnesseth that for sum of Four thousand five hundred
pounds of good sweet scented Tobacco and caske said Powell Stamper doth hereby release to John Lewis the tract of land containing One hundred acres
In presence of HUMPHREY JONES,   Powell Stamper
        RICHD. PERROT, DAVID D GEORGE
At a Court held for Middlesex County the 3d day of July 1711
Powell Stamper came into Court and acknowledged this Lease and Release to John Lewis
which is admitted to Record MARY also the Wife of said Powell appeared and being first
examined freely relinquished her right of Dower in the land which is hereby certified
 KNOW ALL MEN by these presents that I Powell Stamper am bound unto John Lewis in
sum of nine thousand pounds of good sweet scented Tobacco and caske this third day of
July 1711.
The Condition of this obligation is such that if Powell Stamper keep all conditions
mentioned in Indenture and if the Wife of said Powell Stamper relinquish her right of
Dower in said land that then the above obligation to be voyd or else to remain
In presence of HUM: JONES,   Powell Stamper
        RD. PERROTT, DAVID D GEORGE

p.   Middlesex County Sct TO ALL KNOW that I EDWARD WILLIAMS of County of
269   PRINCESS ANNE Planter have appointed my loveing friend WILLIAM STANARD
        of Middlesex County gent to be my lawfull Attorney to acknowledge a Lease and

Release of Seventy acres of land in the County aforesaid unto JOHN FOSTER being the land on which I formerly lived confirming what my said Attorney shall doe. In Witness whereof have set my hand and seale this fifth day of Aprill 1708
In presence of MATT: PERRY,   Edward ⌐ Williams
            WILLIAM W JONES; ANDREW ⅋9 TERRY
   March ye 9th Edward Williams acknowledged this to be his hand & seale in presents of us   JOHN HIPKINGS, ANGELLO CUMMINS
   At a Court held for Middlesex County the 7th day of August 1711
The Within Letr. of Attorney was proved in Court by the oaths of Matthew Perry and Andrew Terry and admitted to record.

pp.   THIS INDENTURE made the twenty third and twenty fourth day of November
269-   1708 Between EDWARD WILLIAMS of County of Middlesex Planter of one part and
274   JOHN FOSTER of same County Taylor Witnesseth that Whereas said Edward Wil-
         liams by Indenture dated the day before this date did sell unto said John Foster
land in the County of Middlesex containing Seventy acres of land bound beginning at a Corner Hickory of Mr. WILLIAM DOWNINGs land standing by the side of the Dragon Swamp and thence running along said Downings land North East to a small Corner white oake being the beginning of said Downings lands thence North East to a Corner Hickroy of Mr. JOHN WORTHAMs land thence continueing same course Southwest binding upon Worthams land to the Draggon Swamp continueing the same course to the maine run of said Swamp thence up the Run to the place it began the said land being granted to Edward Williams by Patent dated the twentyeth day of October 1691 and also a parcell of land adjoyning said plantation which was conveyed by WILLIAM DOWNING JUNR. to said Edward Williams by Deed dated the tenth day of February 1692/3 the same land being bound beginning at the North side of the PATH which goes from the planta-tion of Mr. John Wortham deced to the now dwelling plantation of Mr. William Downing Senior and soe along his Spring Branch to the corner tree by his own old feild being a White oake and down the line to the same path to the beginning To Hold the said land unto said John Foster for term of Six months to the end that by virtue of the Statute for transferring uses into possession said John Foster may be in actuall possession Now This Indenture Witnesseth that said Edward Williams for sum of Twenty five pounds lawfull money of Virginia doth release unto him the said John Foster his heires all the aforesaid Plantation and land
In presence of WILLIAM W CARTER JUNR.,   Edward ⌐ Williams
           JAMES ⌐ MACKEY, WIL. STANARD
   At a Court held for Middlesex County the 7th day of August 1711
William Stanard came this day into Court and by virtue of a Letter of Attorney from Ed-ward Williams presented and acknoweldged this Lease and Release to John Foster which is admitted to record
   This day also appeared WILLIAM BRISTOW and by virtue of a letter of Attorney from CATHARINE WILLIAMS the Wife of said Edward relinquished her right of Dower in the lands conveyed which is hereby certified
   KNOW ALL MEN by these presents that I CATHERINE WILLIAMS Wife of Edward Wil-liams of County of Middlesex do appoint my well beloved Friend William Bristoe to appear in Middx. County Court and acknowledge all my right unto John Foster unto a parcell of land conveyed by my husband Edward Williams In Witness whereof I have set my hand and seale this twenty fourth day of November 1708
In presence of JOHN BARNETT,   Katherine + Williams
           HENRY H BALL, ANNE A BARNETT

At a Court held for Middlesex County the 7th day of August 1711
Proved in Court by the oathes of John Barnett and Anne his Wife and admitted to record

p.   KNOW ALL MEN by these presents that I JAMES WALKER of County of Middlesex
274   have appointed my loveing Brother RICHD. WALKER my lawfull Attorney with
        full power to adjust all accounts whatsoever depending between me and all per-
sons in the Colony of Virginia and to receive all debts and also in my name to sue or
prosecute any person for any debts belonging unto me. In Witness I have set my hand
and seal the 24th day of July in the tenth year of the Reign of our Sovereign Lady Anne
1711.
In presence of WM. KILPIN,   James Walker
        CHARLES BISHOP
    At a Court held for Middx. County the 7th day of August 1711
This Letter of Attorney was proved in Court by the oaths of ye witnesses to it which is
admitted to record

p.   KNOW ALL MEN by these presents that we WM. KILPIN, OLIVER SEGAR and WIL-
275   LIAM STANARD Gent are bound unto our Sovereign Lady Anne in sum of ten
        thousand pounds of Tobo this 7th day of August 1711.
The Condition of this obligation is such that Whereas William Kilpin hath obtained a
Lycence to keep an ORDINARY at URBANNA if said William Kilpin doth constantly provide good and cleanly lodgeing and dyatt for travellers and Stableage fodder and provender or pastureage as the season shall require for their horses dureing the term of
one whole year from the day hereof and not suffer any unlawfull gameing or on the
Sabbath day suffer any person to tipple more than is necessary that then this obligation to be voyd or else to stand
                                            W. Kilpin
                                    Oliver Segar   Wil. Stanard
    At a Court held for Middx. County the 7th day of August 1711
This bond was presented in Court and acknowledged by the Subscribers to it and admitted to record

pp.   KNOW ALL MEN by these presents that I WILLIAM GORDON of Middx. County Mer-
275-   cht. have appointed THOMAS McCLELLAN & BRIDGETT CHARLTON GORDON both of
276   URBANNA in Rappa River in Virga my true and lawfull Attorneys in my name to
        demand and receive from all persons with the Governt. of Virga. and MARILAND
all and singular debts, money, slaves, cattle and demands whatsoever of said Constituant
which shall be oweing and (if occasion be) to appear in all Courts to answer to all matters touching the premises and generally to doe whatsoever said Constituent himselfe
might do if present. In Witness whereof I have put my hand and Seale this Nineteenth
day of October 1710
In presence of CHR. ROBINSON,   Willm. Gordon
        JAMES RISK
    At a Court held for Middlesex County the 7th day of August 1711
This Letter of Attorney was proved in Court by the oaths of the Wittnesses to it which is
admitted to record

pp.   KNOW ALL MEN by these presents that wee ELIZA. MULLINS, CHARLES LEE and
276-   WILLIAM GARDNER of Middx. County are bound unto MATTHEW KEMP gent first
277   in the Commission of the peace for the above County in sum of one hundred and
        fifty pounds this 4th day of September 1711.

The Condition of this obligation is such that Elizabeth Mullins Executrix of WILLIAM MULLINS deced who at a Court held for the above County the 4th day of September 1711 obtained a Probate of the last Will and Testament of said Wm. Mullins deced Now if said Elizabeth Mullins shall at all times hereafter fullfill the said Will and fully satisfy all Legacys then the above obligation to be voyd otherwise to remain

In presence of us THOMAS HENMAN,   Eliza. ℞ Mullins
    WIL. STANARD   Charles Lee   Willm. W/Gardner

At a Court held for Middlesex County the 4th day of September 1711
This bond was acknowledged in Court and admitted to record

pp.   Middlesex County Sct CHRISTOPHER ROBINSON and JOHN ROBINSON two of her
277-   Majts. Justices of the Peace for said County to the Keeper of her Majts. Goale for
278   the said County greeting. Wee send you herewith the body of Capt. GEORGE WOR-
THAM who was this day brought before us on suspission of his felonious Mur-
thering one BENJA. DAVIS of the County who on his examination saith that Benja. Davis aforesaid after some Controversy assaulted him the said Worthm who haveing dropt his Cane drew his Sword in his hand in defence and says that the said Davis presses so hard on him that he ran on the point of his the said Worthams Sword he the said Wortham being prevented from flying from the said Davis by the Corner of an house and an old Arbor also by the Oaths of DUDLEY JOLLEY and WILLIAM CHESHEIRE it appears that said Davis received a Wound by the said Capt. Worthams Sword the Sword then being in the said Worthams hand and Wm. Chesheire saith he saw nothing to hinder the said Wortham from flying from the said Davis by which evidence also appeares that said Wound was the occasion of his the said Davis's death these are therefore in behalfe of our Sovereign Lady the Queen to command you that you immediately you receive the said Capt. George Wortham and him safely keep in your Goale untill he shall be thence delivered by the due order of her Majts. Laws hereof faile not as you will answer the Contemp at your perrill. Given under our hands this 15th day of Septr 1711

You are also to make returne hereof   Christopher Robinson
  to the Next Court helden for this County   Jno. Robinson

Memo that on the within mentioned 14th day of September the within mentioned Capt. George Wortham was by he the within named Gaoler reced and detaint in the Goale of this County for the Cause therein mentioned and that the same is the true and only cause of the detention of the sd Capt. George Wortham dated 22 Septr 1711.
                  p me   JNO. CURTIS S S M C

At a Court held for Middx. County ye 22d day of Septr 1711
The within Mittimus and ret were admitted to record

p.   Middlesex County Sct. CHRISTOPHER ROBINSON and JOHN ROBINSON two of her
278   Majtys Justices of the Peace for the County aforesaid to the Sheriff of the said
     County greeting. Whereas Capt. GEORGE WORTHAM of this County was on Satur-
day last being the Fifteenth instant brought before us the said Justices and charged with the Murther of one BENJA. DAVIS of said County and Whereas to us the aforesd Justices it appeared that the Offence committed by aforesaid Capt. George Wortham was Criminall and only tryable in the Generall Court therefore wee the said Justices did then committ the aforesaid Capt. George Wortham to the Goale of this County Wherefore wee the said Justices require you and doe hereby strictly command you in her Majts. name that immediately on Sight hereof you Summons the Justices of the County to meet on Saturday next being the 22d instant by ten of the Clock in the morning at the Court house of said County to hold a Court for examineing the Offence committed by said Capt. George Wortham and also to doe as by Law enjoyned hereof you are not to faile as you

will answer the contrary at your perrill. Given under our hands and seales this 20th day of Septr 1711.

    The within mentioned Warrant   Christopher Robinson
     Executed by me   OLIVER SEGAR SMC   Jno. Robinson
     September 21 1711
   At a Court held for Middlesex County ye 22d day of Septr 1711
The Within mentioned Warrant and return are admitted to record

p.   Middx. County Sct Capt. GEORGE WORTHAM of this County being brot this day be-
279   fore us MATTHEW KEMP, CHRISTOPHER ROBINSON and JOHN ROBINSON three of
      her Majts. Justices of the Peace for this County for the suspicon of Murther of
BENJA. DAVIS late of this County who being examined saith, that on Thursday last being the 13th Instant and Muster day where he the sd Wortham mustered his troop after he had done mustering the people went to running of Races and won and left some Syder and he was desired to stay and drink part with them & some body asked him whether WM. MATTHEWS had Stole his Mare or no which Mare he had attached and he answered Yes and then within Benja. Davis told him he was an honest man and took his Mare where he could find her and that he the said Capt. Wortham was a Rouge and a Knave and gave him the said Wortham a great deale of ill language and then the said Wortham left him and went into the house haveing his Sword by his Side all the while and after he had been in the house some small time Davis came in and gave the said Wortham more ill language but he persuaded him to be quiate and he was soe till heared a man a nocking in the prison and then asked him who was such a block head to put that man there whither such a Pupey as he or know he the said Wortham answered it was Mr. Christopher Robinson as he was Informed that committed him and that could answer it be believed upon that Davis said Mr. Christopher Robinson was a blockhead and a pupey and that all the Justices were fooles and did not know their Duty and then he the said Wortham desired him to be quiet againe and use better language but he still kept raleing like a Mad man and he the said Capt. Wortham saith further that he held up his Cane and pointed towards him and said Ben dont rave so upon which Benja. Davis drew his Sword and made a blow at the said Worthams head who fended it of with his Cane and got up to flee from him and he made another blow at him and that he defendd with his Cane and fleed to the door to have got his horse out of the mans hands that held him there but Davis persued soe fast out of the door that he could not get to his horse and he jumped out of the door and dropt his Cane and Davis still followed him and repeated his blows at him upon which the said Wortham drew his Sword and desired him to stand of and not persue him asked if he had a mind to murder him and he prest hard upon him swearing and raveing like a mad man and he the said Wortham still drawing back from him and asked him if he had a mind to murder him whereupon Davis flew at him at once and run upon the point of his Sword & run it into his left brest and the said Wor-tham saith that he made noe pass at him & that beat his Sword down as he was guarding himselfe and then run upon the point of it and the said Capt. Wortham being asked what prevented his flying from the said Davis says that the Corner of the house and an old Arbor were in his Way

   At a Court held for Middlesex County the 22d day of Septr 1711
This Examination of Capt. Worthams relateing to the Murther of Benja. Davis is admitted to record

pp.   Middlesex County SS WILLIAM CHESHEIRE of this County aged about twenty
280-   being sworn to give his Evidence concerning the death of BENJAMINE DAVIS (in
283   behalfe of our Sovereign Lady) saith that on Thursday the 13th instant a little

after Sun Sett he came from his worke to the Ordinary at the Court House in this County where he saw Capt. GEORGE WORTHAM and BENJAMINE DAVIS and severall other people togather at the end of the Ordinary where he heard them in an argument about a Mare that Capt. Wortham had attached belonging to one WILLIAM MATTHEWS and heard Benjamine Davis tell Capt. Wortham he had done the thing that was unfair for that he had attached the mans mare that he had no more right to then himselfe had whereupon Capt. Wortham desired him to be pacyfied and not to trouble his head about that for it did not concerne him and the Depo. further saith that RICHARD PAFFAT one of the Company asked Capt. Wortham to goe into the house and smoake a pipe & drink a pot and then they should be free of Davis his noise and then they two went in and some others with them and the deponent and Benjamine Davis and some others staid without & in some time they went in after them and after severall arguments they began to talk of the man in prison and Davis said that he had four men of his mind he would breake the prison door open and lett him out afterwards he asked for the key severall times to let him out and said he would stand to it when he had done whereupon Capt. Wortham desired him to be easy & to be pacyfied (as he had done severall times before) and not to concern himself with that did not belong to him but that the more he endeavoured to pacyfie him the worse Davis was and said that they were Loggardheads and Pupes that put the man in prison whereas Capt. Wortham seemed to be angry with him and bid him hold his tongue but Davis still persisting in his talk Capt. Wortham said some word (which the Depo. saith he hath forgott) which disturbed Benjamine Davis who repeated it Severall times after whereupon Capt. Wortham said Sure Benja. it is not come to that that I must be afraid to speak for you and with that bid him hold his tongue and talk noe more of it and held up his Cane and said he was like his Uncle PRITCHARD and Davis answered that if he was like his Uncle Prichard he would stand by his Uncle Prichard till he dyed and then Capt. Wortham held his Cane towards him again and bid him be pacyfied and Benja. Davis seeing him hold up his Cane haveing his Sword in his hand struck it at him the sd Wortham with the Scabbard on and apprehending that Capt. Wortham threatened him with his Cane he drew his Sword and struck at him the said Wortham severall times which he defended with his Cane till he either accidently or willfully left it whereupon he drew his Sword and held it right against Benjamine Davis and bid him stand of but Davis still endeavouring to get a blow at him followed him close up & at last turned from him and came towards the Depo. haveing put up his Sword and said Capt. Wortham I did not think to do you any harme & the said Davis in a crying tone said he was a dead man and opening his Shirt to look at something the Deponent saith he saw some blood upon his Shirt and Davis said prithee Will fetch my horse and that he went to the Arbor for his horse but he was gone soe he returned presently and before he come to him againe he saw him fall right upon his face and that he & DUDLEY JOLLEY took him up & that he then bled at his Mouth and nose they would have set him down but he seemed to be willing rather to lye down and they let him lye and Dudley Jolley took his Shirt and tore it to see where the blood came from and found a wound under his left brest which the Depont. believed was done by Capt. Worthams Sword and being asked he saith that he saw nothing to hinder him the said Wortham from flying further from the said Davis he also saith that Davis lived about two hours after and then dyed and further the depo. saith not. Sworn this 15th day of Septr 1711 before
                        CHRISTOPHER ROBINSON
                JOHN ROBINSON   Wm. + Chesheir
    The before mentioned Will Chesheir further saith that Capt. George Wortham desired Benja. Davis to be quiet severall times and gave him all the good words he could and that he did not perceive any Enmity or malice in the said Wortham towards the said Davis and particularly that Capt. Wortham had some discourse with the said Davis about being

his Overseer a little before and that when Capt. Wortham drew his Sword he did not perceive that he made any offer at Davis but only to defend himselfe from said Davis and further saith that he thinks Capt. Wortham could not have fled from the said Davis without danger of being killed and further saith not

Taken before us this 15th Septr 1711   Wm. ⊥ Chesheir
    CHR. ROBINSON   JOHN ROBINSON

JACOB STIFFE came before us and said he was in Company with Capt. Wortham and Benja. Davis on Thursday last and heard them have some discourse about a Mare also about a man in the prison and that Davis gave Capt. Wortham a great deal of bad language and that Capt. Wortham gave no hard words nor did not seem to be angry with him and had some discourse with him about Davis being his Overseer and that he verily believes that Capt. Wortham bore him noe malice that that he left them very quiet and further saith not.

Taken before us this 15th Septr 1711   Jacob Stiffe
    CHR. ROBINSON   JOHN ROBINSON

Middlesex County Sct DUDLEY JOLLEY of this County aged forty three years being sworn to give his Evidence concerning he death of BENJA. DAVIS of this County saith that on Thursday the 13th instant he was at the Court House of this County where Capt. Wortham say something about a Mare that WILLIAM MATTHEWS had stolen whereto Benja. Davis made answer and said that Matthews had done like an honest man and what he would have done himselfe and he saith this was before night by the Ordinary and this Deponent further saith that afterwards he came into the house abt an hour after and that then he heard them have some words about a man that was a Prisoner and that Benja. Davis said that if he had the key of the prison or could get it he would let him out and he thinks he heard him say that if he had four men like himself he would take him out and severall other words which he does not remember and then that he the said Benja. Davis drew his Sword in the Scabbard and struck at the said Capt. Wortham who defended himselfe with his Cane and then Davis drew his Sword out of the Scabbard and struck at Capt. Wortham againe with his naked Sword or rather a hanger which he againe defendd with his Cane and stept back and then his Cane fell down whereupon he stept back and drew his Sword and helt it out before him and bid Benja. Davis stand off who struck at him again & that Capt. Wortham told Davis that he had a Sword as well as he and therefore bid him stand off who still followed him till he made a sudden stopp and said that he was wounded or he had his death or to that effect and he further saith that after that he saw Davis open his bosome and said something that he doe not well remember and about a quarter of an hour afterwards he fell down and then the Depot. went to him and saw bloud upon his Shirt and cloathes which he supposed to issue from some wound wherefore he tore his the said Davis his shirt to look for it and found under his left brest a wound which he took to be a prick of Capt. Worthams rapier and that he the depot. and WILLIAM CHESHEIR took up the said Davis and set him up against the house and left him leaning his head against the other man as he supposed dead and further this Deponent saith that to the best of his remembrance this is the truth of the case but that he cannot be positive in it because he was something in drink and further saith not.

Sworn before us this 15th day Septr 1711   Dudley ∂ Jolley
    CHR. ROBINSON   JNO. ROBINSON

The aforesaid Dudley Jolley further saith that Capt. George Wortham desired Benja. Davis to be quiet and gave him all the good words he could and that he did not perceive any Enmity in said Worthan towards said Davis

This is also delivered before us 15th day   Dudley ꝺ Jolley
        Chr. Robinson   Jno. Robinson
    At a Court held for Middx. County the 22 Septr 1711
    The Deposition of Dudley Jolley is admitted to record

p.   KNOW ALL MEN by these presents that wee GEORGE WORTHAM, JOHN GRYMES,
283   WM. ROAN, WM. CALLANONE, RALPH BAKER and ROBERT BROOKING stand bound
          unto our Sovereign Lady the Queen in sum of Five hundred pounds Sterl. money
this 22d day of September 1711
    The Condition of this obigation is such that Whereas George Wortham is by the Judg-
ment of this Court to have his Tryall in the Generall Court on Suspetion of his mur-
thering BENAJA. DAVIS of the said County Now if said George Wortham shall appear on
the fourth day of said next Generall Court and shall there abide by the Judgment of said
Generall Court as they shall award that then this obligation to be voyd or else to remain
In presence of THOMAS MEACHEM,   George Wortham
        JNO. CURTIS, WILL. STANARD   John Grymes   Wm. Roan
                                            William Callanone   Ralph Baker
                                            Robert Brooking
    At a Court held for Middx. County the 22d day of September 1711
    This Bond was acknowledged by the severall Subscribers to it and admitted to record

pp.   KNOW ALL MEN by these presents that wee OLIVER SEGAR and HARRY BEVERLEY
283-   of County of Middlesex are bound unto our Sovereign Lady the Queen in sum of
284   four thousand pounds of good sound sweet scented Tobacco and caske this
          second day of Janry. 1711.
    The Condition of this obigiation is such that if Oliver Segar Sheriff shall collect the
publick and County leveys and faithfully pay to the Creditors for whom they were
raised as same is ordered by Act of Assembly begun ye 23d day of October 1705 that then
the above obligation to be voyd or else to stand
In presence of JNO. PRICE,   Oliver Segar
        JOHN SEGAR   Harry Beverley
    Acknowledged in Court the 2d day of Janry. by the Subscribers to it and admitted to
record

p.   KNOW ALL MEN by these presents that wee PEN: PERROTT, OLIVER SEGAR and
284   ALEXANDER GRAVES are bound unto RICHARD PERROTT Gent the sum of one
          thousand pounds Sterl. this 6th day of January 1711.
    The Condition of this obligation is such that Whereas Penelope Perrott hath appealed
from a Judgment of the Middx. County Court obtained against her by Richard Perrott
Now if Penelope Perrott shall appear on said 8th day of next Genll. Court and prosecute
her said appeale and if cast satisfie the principall debt and costs with fifteen p cent that
then this obligation to be voyd or else to stand
In presence of EDWARD WALFORD,   Pen: ꝗꝗ Perrott
        WIL. STANARD ClCur   Oliver Segar   Alexander Graves
    Acknowledged in Court the 6th day of January ( ) and admitted to record

p.   KNOW ALL MEN by these presents that wee JAMES MEACHAM, EDWARD CLARKE
285   and JACOB STIFFE are bound unto JOHN SMITH Gent first in Comission of the
          peace for said County in sum of one hundred pounds Sterl this 6th day of Jany
1711. The Condition of this obligation is such that if James Meacham shall truely pay
unto JONATHAN JOHNSON Orphan of JOHN JOHNSON deced all such Estates as shall appear

to be due as soon as he the said Orphan shall attain to lawfull age & keep harmless the
Justices from said Estate that then this obligation to be voyd otherwise to be
In presence of EDWARD WALFORD,   James Meacham
          WIL. STANARD ClCur   Jacob Stiffe   Edwd. E Clarke
     At at Court held for Middlesex County the 6th day of January 1711
This bond was acknowledged in open Court by the Subscribers to it and admitted to
record

pp.   KNOW ALL MEN by these presents that wee ELIZA. HICKEY, JNO. HARDEE & THO-
285-   MAS KIDD are bound unto MATTHEW KEMP Gent First in Commission of the peace
286   for Middx. County in sum of one hundred pounds Sterl. money of great Brittaine
             this fifth day of February 1711.
  The Condition of this obligation is such that Whereas Admon. of the Estate of JOHN
HICKEY deced is by the Court granted unto Eliza. Hickey Now if said Eliza. Hickey shall
return a true inventory and render a true account of all the said Estate and true payment make of said Estate to whom it shall belong that then this obligation to be voyd or
else to stand   Eliza. + Hickey
                                                Jno. Hardee   Tho: Kidd
     Acknowledged in Court by the Subscribers to it the 5th day of February 1711 and ad-
mitted to record

p.   KNOW ALL MEN by these presents that wee MARY CARTER, HENRY GOODLOE &
286   JACOB PRESSON of Middx. County are bound unto JOHN SMITH Gent first in Comis-
             sion of the peace for the said County in sum of three hundred pounds Sterl. this
5th day of February 1711.
  The Condition of this obligation is such that Mary Carter Executrix of WILLIAM CAR-
TER deced who obtained a Probate of the last Will and Testament of the said Wm. Carter
deced shall at all times fullfill the said Will and performe all the Law enjoyns in such
cases that then the above obligation to be void otherwise to remain
In presence of us JNO. CURTIS,   Mary 9 Carter
          Wil. STANARD   Henry Goodlo   Jacob Presson
     Acknowledged in Court the 5th day of February 1711 and admitted to record

pp.   THIS INDENTURE made the 4th September 1711 Between WILLIAM BROOKES of
286-   County of Middx. Planter of one part and JAMES MACTYRE of said County Planter
288   Witnesseth that said William Brookes for a valuable consideration hath sold unto
             said James Mactyre all that parcell of land now in Occupation of said William
Brookes in County of Middx. bounded with the land of DOCTOR STAPLETON deced, RICHD.
ATTWOOD & CORDWELLs Spring Branch containing Fifty acres of land
In presence of JOHN OWEN (1711)   Wm. ⊕ Brookes
          MARY GRAVES, HANAH HH MACTYRE
     At a Court held for Middlesex County the 5th day of February 1711
William Brookes came into Court and acknowledged the above Deed to James Mactyre
which is admitted to record ELIZA. also the Wife of said Wm. came into Court and being
first examined relinquished her right of Dower
     KNOW ALL MEN by these presents that I William Brookes of Middx. County am bounden
unto James Mactyre of same County in Quantity of four thousand pounds of good sound
merchantable Swt. scented Tobacco & caske this 4th day of September 1711.
  The Condition of this obligation is such that if William Brookes shall at all times hereafter keep all the articles mentioned in Indenture which ought to be kept that then this
obligation to be void otherwise to stand

In presence of JOHN OWEN (1711)   Wm. ⊕ Brookes
    MARY GRAVES, HANAH ⊢⊣ MACTYRE
  At a Court held for Middlesex County the 5th day of February 1711
This Bond was acknowledged by the Subscriber which is admitted to record

pp.   THIS INDENTURE made the twenty second day of September 1711 Between ROGER
288- JONES of County of Middlesex of one part and ROBERT CARTER of County of LAN-
291   CASTER Esqr. Witnesseth that said Roger Jones for sum of Sixty pounds lawfull
        money of Great Brittaine sold unto said Robert Carter his heires forever land in
County of Middx. containing One hundred and fifty acres formerly granted to THOMAS
DUDLEY & WILLIAM ELLIOTT by Patent dated the 20th Aprill 1690 and since conveyed
down to the said Roger Jones bounded Beginning at the Corner Red oake on the Green
Branch Corner tree of EDWIN THACKERs land and running up along the said Green
Branch to a certain corner tree thence South East along a line of marked trees to the
land of the said Edwin Thackers thence along said Thackers land by an old crooked line
of marked trees to ye place where it began
In presence of THOMAS MACHEN,   Rogr. Jones
    DANLL. CARTER, PATRICK ⅄ DAGLE
  At a Court held for Middx. County the 5th day of February 1711
Roger Jones Gentl. came this day into Court and acknowledged the Deed to the Honble
Robert Carter Esqr. which is admitted to record MARY JONES also the Wife of said Roger
Jones came into Court and being first examined freely relinquished her Right of Dower
in said land which is hereby certyfied
  Memorandum that Livery Seizin & possession of the within given by Roger Jones unto
Robert Carter in the presence of us
THO: MACHEN   DANLL. CARTER   JOHN Ɪ DUDLE   FRANCES ╅ GRASON
  KNOW ALL MEN by these presents that I Roger Jones of the Parish of Christ Church in
Middlesex County am bound unto Robert Carter of Lancaster County Esqr. in sume of one
hundred and twenty pounds lawfull money of great Brittain this 22d day of September
1711. The Condition of this obligation is such that if Roger Jones shall truely keep at all
times all the Covenants expressed in Deed and further said Roger Jones and his Wife
acknowledge the said Deed before some Court held for the County of Middx. that then
this obligation to be void otherwise to stand
In presence of THO: MACHEN,   Roger Jones
    DANLL. CARTER, PATRICK ⅄ DAGLE
  At a Court held for Middx. County the 5th day of February 1711
Roger Jones acknowledged this bond which is admitted to record

p.   February the 5th 1711 Mr. HARRY BEVERLEY. A: Appear my Attorney in Middx.
291   Court in all actions I am concerned in   PAUL THILMAN
    Recr Test Lettr. Attorney

p.   KNOW ALL MEN by these presents that wee PAUL THILMAN & WILLIAM JONES
291   are bound unto JOHN HICKEY in penall sum of one thousand nine hundred and
       two pounds of good Tobaco this 19th day of March 1706.
  The Condition of this obligation is such that if Paul Thilman and William Jones shall at
all times keep harmless John Hicky from all troubles that may accrue by reason that
said John Hickey paid ELIZABETH SUMMERS the Daughter of ye JOHN SUMMERS deced
the sume of nine hundred & fifty one pounds of good sweet scented Tobacco being due
to her the said Elizabeth Summers parte of her Fathers Estate by order of Middx. County

Court that then this obligation to be void otherwise to stand
Witness RICHARD DANIELL   Paul Thilman
                                                  Wm. Jones
    At a Court held for Middx. County the first day of April 1712
Presented in Court and acknowledged by Paul Thilman and admitted to record

pp.   THIS INDENTURE made the thirteenth day of May 1689 and in the fifth year of
292- the Reign of our Sovereign Lord James the second between JOHN FURRELL of
294   the Parish of Christ Church in County of Middx. and ANNE his Wife of one part
      and ROBERT CLARKE of the Parish and County aforesaid Witnesseth that said
John Furrell and Anne his Wife for the full quantity of two thousand pounds of good
and merchantable sweet scented Tobacco and Caske do sell unto said Robert Clarke his
heires One hundred acres of land it being part of Five hundred and ninety three acres
of land formerly granted to JOHN KITCHINS and GEORGE HOOPER and for want of due
seating and planting was by them deserted and by an Order of the Genll. Court in November 1678 said land was granted to Mr. EDWARD THOMAS and by said Edward Thomas
conveyed to THOMAS TOSELEY by Sale dated the 21st day of June 1680 and by the said
Thomas Toseley conveyed to said John Furrell by Sale dated the ( ) day of ( ) and
bounded begining at an old white oake stump and white oake marked by Corner trees of
JOHN JADWIN and WILLIAM BLAISE and runing thence by an old line of marked trees
North East to a corner Hickory on the side of a hill and by a Valley thence South West
by a marked line to a branch thence down the branch its winds and turnes to the land
of DODES MINOR to a marked line and finally thence North East to the first specified
station only excepting a peice of land joyning to the said Branch fifty foot in length
and forty foot in breadth opposite to the place where the said John Furrell shall set his
TAN YARD dureing the time of the said Tan Yard shall stand or remaine there the said
Furrell shall have the use of the said peice of land
In presence of us EDWARD THOMAS,   John I Furrell
    MAURICE COCKE   Anne   Furrell
    At a Court held for Middlesex County the 13th day of May 1689
Then personally appeared John Furrell and in open Court did acknowledge ye above
Deed to be his act and deed ANNE FURRELL also came into Court and being privately
examined acknowledged said Deed to be her act and deed
           Copia Test   WIL STANARD ClCur   Test J. VAUSE Cl Cur 89
    KNOW ALL MEN by these presents that I ROBERT CLARKE of County of Middlesex have
for the sum of Seventeen hundred pounds of good sweet scented Tobacco & Caske paid
by JOHN MERCY of the County of ESSEX do sell all my right to the within Deed and the
One hundred acres of land to said John Mercy his heires forever To Hold the same and I
doe further bind myself that I will togather with SARAH CLARKE my Wife acknowledge
these presents in open Court. In Witness whereof I have set my hand and seale this 6
day of May 1712.
In presence of EDWARD PENDERGRASS,   Robert Clarke
    ELIZABETH + PENDERGRASS
    At a Court held for Middlesex County the 6th day of May 1712
Robert Clarke came into Court and acknowledged the above assignment to be his act and
deed to John Mercy which is admitted to record SARAH also the Wife of said Robert
appeared in Court & being examined relinquished her right of Dower to the land which
is hereby certyfied

p.   KNOW ALL MEN by these presents that wee OLIVER SEGAR, RALPH WORMELEY
295 and JOHN PRICE Gent. of County of Middx. are bound unto our Sovereign Lady

Queen Anne in sum of one thousand pounds Sterl. this 6th day of May 1712.

The Condition of this obligation is such that Whereas Oliver Segar is by a Commission from the Honble the Lt. Governor appointed Sheriff of the abovesaid County for this insueing year Now if said Oliver Segar will at all times render unto the Auditor such account of all her Majts. Revenues in said County dureing the time of his Sherivalty and also due payment of all publick and County dues and diligently find out the true quantity of land held in the aforesaid County and returne a true & perfect list or rent-role of the same to her Majts. Auditor and full performance make of all things relateing to the office of Sheriff that then this obligation to be voyd or else to stand
In presence of WIL. STANARD ClCur   Oliver Segar
                           Ralph Wormeley Jno. Price

pp. 295-296   March the 31st 1712. A true and just Account of JOHN ARRENTONs Debts paid by Order of Court p me the Subscriber: To MINOR MINOR, to JOHN CURTIS, to Capt. ROBERT DANIELL, to Mr. EDMOND HAMERTON, to ELIZABETH HOUL, to RICE JONES, to THOMAS BIRD; to MATHEW COX, to Collo. GAWIN CORBIN; to HENRY WEBBER, to Mr. WIL. STANARD, to JOHN HARDEE, to HENRY HAYES, to WILLIAM WHELER, to Sectr. fees paid MR. KEMP, to my own accompt; to Levies Total 6188 paid 6158 Estate
At a Court held for Middx. County the 6th day of May 1712
JOHN MERCY Administrator of the Estate of JOHN ARRINGTON presented this account to his administration in Court which is admitted to record.

p. 296   W. STANARD October ye 21, 1711. This comes to request you to set down the Inventory of ROBERT DUDLEYs Estate 2 steares of 4 years ould & 1 heifer of 4 years ould   Yr humble Sert.   ELIZA: ELLIOT
To Mr. WILLM. STANARD
At Court held for Middlesex County the 3d June 1713
This Additional Inventory of Robert Dudleys Estate is admitted to record

pp. 296-298   THIS INDENTURE made the fourth day of May 1712 and in the Eleaventh year of the Reign of our Sovereign Lady Anne Between GEORGE STAPLETON of Middx. County of one part and JOHN MOSELEY of other part Witnesseth that for sum of two thousand six hundred pounds of good sweet scented tobacco and caske paid by said John Mosely to above George Stapleton hath granted unto said John Moseley forty acres of land bindeing upon the White Oak Swamp in Middx. County bought by THOMAS STAPLETON decest of HENRY NICHOLLS as by Deed bindeing upon DAVID GEORGEs land and also CANADAYs land
In presence of ALEXANDER GRAVES,   Geo: Stapleton
      WILL: DANIELL, JAMES MEACHAM
At a Court held for Middlesex County the 1st day of July 1712
George Stapleton came into Court and acknowledged the above Deed to John Moseley which is admitted to record
KNOW ALL MEN by these presents that I George Stapleton am bound unto John Moseley in the sume of five thousand two hundred pounds of good sweet scented Tobacco & Caske this 4th day of May 1712.

The Condition of this obligation is such that if the above bound George Stapleton at all times keep all covenants mentioned in certain Indenture to John Moseley that then this obligation to be void or else to remaine
In presence of ALEXANDER GRAVES,   Geo: Stapleton
      JAMES MEACHAM, WILL: DANIELL

At a Court held for Middx. County the first day of July 1712
George Stapleton acknowledged this bond which is admitted to record

pp.   KNOW ALL MEN by these presents that we JAMES MEACHAM, ALEXANDER GRAVES
298-   & JACOB STIFFE of Middlesex County are bound unto CHRISTOPHER ROBINSON Gent
299   First in Comission of the peace ffor the above County in sum of three hundred
        pounds Sterl. this 2d day of September 1712.
The Condition of this obligation is such that if James Meacham Executor of JOHN
MEACHAM deced who at Court on the 2d day of September 1712 obtained a Probate of the
last Will and Testament of said John Meacham deced shall at all times fullfill the said
Will and fully satisfy all Legacys Expressed that then this obligation to be voyd other-
wise to remaine
In presence of J. HARDEE,   James Meacham
                              Alexander Graves   Jacob Stiffe
   Acknowledged in Middx. County Court the 2d day of September 1712 by the Subscribers
to it and admitted to record

p.   KNOW ALL MEN by these presents that wee GEORGE BARRICK & THOMAS MACHEN
299   and JACOB STIFFE are bound unto JOHN SMITH Gent first in Comission of peace
        for County aforesaid in sum of five hundred pounds Sterling this third day of
February 1712.
The Condition of this obligation is such that if George Barrick shall truely pay unto
CHRISTIPHER KILBEE Orphan of WILLIAM KILBEE deced all Estate as shall appear to be
due to said Orphan as soon as he shall attaine to lawfull age and keep harmless the Jus-
tices from said Estate that then this obligation to be voyd otherwise to stand
In presence of WILLIAM GRAY,   Geo: Barrick
        WIL. STANARD   Tho: Machen   Jacob Stiffe
   Acknowledtged in Court the 3d day of February 1712 by the Subscribers to it and admitted to record

p.   JAMES MEACHAM Executor of the Will of JOHN MEACHAM deced who was lately
299   one of the Admrs. of JOHN BRAME deced Charges the Estate of the said deced
         Brame as followeth: To paid NICHO. BRAME Judgmt. paid Sheriff; paid JOHN
ALDIN; to Genl Fee paid Mr. HARRY BEVERLEY, paid JOHN BRAME his part; paid RICHARD
BRAME his part, to cattle returned and 1 Musquet to ye surviveing Adminex. To ballance
due the Orphans of Brame yet in my hands 181 Tobo p JAMES MEACHAM Executor of Jno.
Meacham deced late one of ye Admrs. of John Brame deced
   At a Court held for Middx. County the 7th day of April 1713
Produced in Court by James Meacham and admitted to record
                      Truely recorded Test R. HICKMAN D ClCur

p.   Virginia Sct To all Know ye that I THOMAS WILLIAMSON of the County of Albe-
300   marle in the precinct of Currotuck have appointed my loveing friend THOMAS
        ELLIOTT of Middx.County to be my lawfull Attorney to acknowledge a Lease and
Release for One hundred acres of land in Middx. County unto ROBERT DUDLEY of the
County of PRINCESS ANNE in the Colony of Virginia which Deed is dated the 29th and
30th day of May 1713 hereby confirming what my said Attorney shall lawfully do. In
Witness I have set my hand and seal this 1st day of June 1713.
In presence of JNO. CURTIS,   Thomas ⊤ Williamson
        JAMES HACKNEY, WILLIAM /X\CAINE

At a Court held for Middlesex County the 3d day of June 1713
This Letter of Attorney was proved in Court by the Oaths of the Witnesses to it and admitted to record

Test WIL. STANARD ClCur
Truely recorded Test R. HICKMAN D ClCur

pp. THIS INDENTURE made this twenty ninth and thirtieth day of May in the twelfth
300- year of the Reign of our Sovereign Lady Ann and in the year of our Lord 1713
303 Between THOMAS WILLIAMSON of the County of Albamarle in the precinct of
     Currotuck of one part and ROBERT DUDLEY of the County of PRINCESS ANNE in
the Colony of Virginia Witnesseth that Whereas said Thomas Williamson by Indenture
bearing date the day before the date hereof did sell unto said Robert Dudley land in the
County of Middlesex in the Colony of Virginia and beginning at Mr. ROBERT BOODLEs
Swamp and from thence extending to a Swamp comonly called RALPH JOHNSONs branch
and so up along the ROAD that goeth from the FERRY to ye COURT HOUSE includeing all
the land lyeing on that side the branch next to Boodles and also all the land that lyes
between said Boodles Swamp and Ralph Johnsons Branch to the same One hundred acres
of land the said land being formerly conveyed by AUGUSTINE WILLIAMSON to THOMAS
MOUNTJOY of the County of WESTMORELAND Planter by Deed the Sixth day of November
1684 and by the said Thomas Mountjoy sold unto JAMES WILLIAMSON Brother of the
aforesaid Thomas Williamson To Hold the same to said Robert Dudley for the term of one
whole year and that by Virtue of these presents and of the Statute for Transferring uses
into possession the said Robert Dudley might bee in the actuall possession Now this Indenture Witnesseth that said Thomas Williamson for sum of Thirty pounds Sterling
money of great Brittain paid said Thomas Williamson doth confirm unto said Robert
Dudley the same one hundred acres of land
In presence of us JNO. CURTIS,   Thomas + Williams
     WILLIAM /X\ CAINE, JAMES HACKNEY
  At a Court held for Middx. County the 2d day of June 1713
THOMAS ELLIOTT Attorney of Thomas Williamson came into Court & acknowledged the
said Williamsons Deed of lease and release to Robert Dudley which is admitted to record

p.   KNOW ALL MEN by these presents that wee ROBERT CARTER Esqr. and CHRISTO-
303 PHER ROBINSON Gent are bound unto MATTHEW KEMP gent first in commission
     of the peace for County of Middlesex in sum of three hundred pounds Sterl. this
second day of June 1713
  The Condition of the above obligation is that if Robert Carter Esqr. do truely pay unto
JOHN BASHFORD Orphan of SYMON and GRACE BASHFORD deced all such Estate as shall
appear to be due as soon as he shall attain to lawfull age and keep the Justices from all
troubles that may arise about the Estate that then the above obligation to be void otherwise to stand
In presence of WIL. STANARD   Robert Carter
                                                     Chr. Robinson
  Acknowledged in Court by the Subscribers to it and ordered to be recorded

p.   KNOW ALL MEN by these presents that I JOHN ROBINSON of TOWN of URBANNA in
303 County of Middlesex (being by Gods Grace bound for England) doe appoint my
     loveing Brother CHRISTOPHER ROBINSON and HARRY BEVERLEY and my Worthy
freind the Honble. Sr: WILLIAM SKIPWITH Barrt. my lawfull Attorneys for me to act in
all matters relateing to any business belonging to me as if I myselfe were here. In Wit-

ness whereof I have set my hand & seale this ninth day of May 1713
Witness   CHARLES BISHOP,   Jno. Robinson
       JAMES RISKE, W. KILPIN
    At a Court held for Middlesex County the second day of June 1713
The above letter of Attorney was this day proved in Court by the oaths of William Kilpin & James Riske Witnesses to it and admitted to record

p.   KNOW ALL MEN by these presents that wee JOHN VIVION, JOHN SMITH gent and
304   WIL. STANARD of Middlesex County gent are bound unto our Sovereign Lady
        Queen Anne in sum of one thousand pounds Sterl. this second day of June 1713.
   The Condition of the above obligation is such that Whereas John Vivion is by Commission from the Honble Lt. Governr: appointed Sheriff of abovesaid County this ensueing year Now if John Vivion Sheriff shall at all times render unto the Auditor a particular account of all her Matys Revenues in said County dureing time of his Sherivalty and also due payment make unto persons appointed to receive the same and that he find out the true quantity of land held in the aforesaid County by any person and returne a true list or rentroll of same that then this obligation to be void or else to remain
In presence of THO: HENMAN,   Jno. Vivion
       CHA: GRYMES   John Smith   Wil: Stanard
    Acknowledged in Court the 2d day of June 1713 and admitted to record

pp.   THIS INDENTURE made this third and fourth day of May 1713 Betweeen JOHN
304-   CURTIS SENR. of County of NORTHUMBERLAND of one part and HARRY BEVERLEY
306   of County of Middlesex of other part Witnesseth that for sum Fifteen hundred
        pounds of Tobacco the said John Curtis hath released unto the said Harry Beverley in his actuall possession by vertue of a bargaine & sale and by force of the Statute for transferring uses into possession and to his heires forever all that parcell of land and swamp containing Thirty one acres lyeing below the DRAGON BRIDGE in Middlesex County in as full manner as it was granted to John Curtis Senr. by Patent dated the nineteenth December 1711
In presence of JNO. CURTIS JUNR.,   Jno. Curtis Senr.
       JOHN SMITH
 At a Court held for Middlesex County the 7th day of July 1713
John Curtis came this day into Court & acknowledged his lease and release to Harry Beverley which is admitted to record

p.   KNOW ALL MEN by these presents that wee DAVID MORGAN, THOMAS SMITH and
306   WILLIAM KIDD of the County of Middlesex are bound unto MATTHEW KEMP Gent
        first in commission of the peace of said County in sum of one hundred pounds
Sterl. money of Great Brittain this 4th day of August 1713.
   The Condition of this obligation is such that Whereas Admon. of the Estate of THOMAS BURKE deced is by the Court granted unto David Morgan by Order of Court Now if said David Morgan shall return a true inventory to next Court and render a true account of all Estate of said deced and payment make of all the said Estate to whom of right it shall belong that then this obligation to be voyd or else to stand
In presence of JNO. CURTIS,   David _M_ Morgan
       WIL: STANARD   Tho: Smith   William _W_ Kidd
    Acknowledged in Court held for Middx. County the 4th day of August 1713 by the Subscribers to it and admitted to record

pp.   BE IT KNOWN that I ROBERT DUDLEY of PRINCESS ANN County appoint WILLIAM
307-   BLACKBORN of the County of Middx. my lawfull Attorney for me to acknowledge
310   a Lease unto JOHN GIBBS of County of Middx. Weaver and I do allow all my said
         Attorney shall do about the premises. In Witness whereof I have set my hand
and seal this 8th day of June 1713.
In presence of THO: MACHEN,   Robert Ꝓ Dudley
         JOHN BERRY, THO: GODIN
   At a Court held for Middlesex County the 7th day of July 1713
The above Letter of Attorney was proved in Court by the oaths of the witnesses to it &
admitted to record
   THIS INDENTURE made the Eighth day of June 1713 Between ROBERT DUDLEY of Princess Anne County gent of one part and JOHN GIBBS of the Parish of Christ Church and
County of Middlesex Weaver of other part Whereas said Robert Dudley by Indenture
dated the Eighth day of June did sell unto John Gibbs a Plantation and lands comonly
called by the name of WILLIAMS OLD PLANTATION containing One hundred acres of
land in Parish of Christ Church and County of Middx. (and being part of a greater tract
of land bought formerly of EDWIN CONWAY by ANDREW WILLIAMS) and now in the
tenure of WILLIAM NEWBERRY being bounded beginning on Mr. Robert Dudleys
Swamp and Mr. ROBERT BOODLEs Swamp and from thence to a Branch comonly called
RALPH JOHNSONs Branch and so along the branch up to ye Road that goeth from the
FERRY to ye COURT HOUSE To Hold the said land that by virtue of the Statute for transferring uses into possession sd John Gibbs might be in actuall possession NOW THIS
INDENTURE WITNESSETH that Robert Dudley for sume of Four thousand pounds of good
sweet scented Tobacco and caske and three thousand nine hundred pounds of like
Tobacco or Nineteen pounds Ten shillings in goods in a Store to him paid by John Gibbs
by Bill and his hand and seal hath granted unto John Gibbs the aforesaid lands
In presence of THO: MACHEN,   Robert Ꝓ Dudley
         JOHN BERRY, THO: GODIN
   At a Court held for Middx. County the 7th day of July 1713
Wm. Blackborne Attorney for Robert Dudley came into Court & acknowledged this his
lease and release to John Gibbs which is admitted to record

pp.   The Estate of JOHN MEACHAM deced who was lately one of the Adminrs. of the
310-   Estate of JOHN BRAME deced is Dr.
311   To paid JOHN ALLDIN by Judgmt; paid WM. STANARD; to Sheriffs fees; to Mr.
         HARRY BEVERLEY a generall fee, to NICHO. BRAME, to THOMAS HILL; to Tobacco
paid Collo. CORBIN; to EDMD. HAMERTON; to CHA: LEE; to MR. SEGAR; to CAPT. WORTHAM;
to halfe of the ballance of 1362 Tobo returned in the Inventory came to hands of said
deced Meacham; to paid to the Widows part of Brames Estate; paid NICHOLAS BRAME, paid
ELIZA. SOWELL, paid MARY SEARS, paid JOHN BRAME, paid ALICE BRAME; paid RICHINS
BRAME, to JOANNA BRAME; to THOMS. BRAME; to JAMES BRAME; by 2 hoggs sold WM.
GARDINER not inventoryed
   In Obedience to an order of Middlesex Court dated the 8th day of July 1713 Wee the
Subscribers mett at the house of James Meacham and there examined stated and settled
all account and differences between James Meacham Executor of John Meacham who
was lately one of the Admors. of John Brame deced and Mary Meacham ye surviving
Adminx. of said John Brame deced and we have allotted the Orphans of the deced Brame
their parts of the said Brames Estate and we doo award that Mary Meecham surviveing
Administrx. of said John Brame deced give the said James Meacham Executor of said
John Meacham Estate a full discharge from the said James Brames Estate and wee doe
also award that the severall orphans above mentioned give the said Mary Meacham

Surviveing Administratrix a full discharge for their parts of their deced Fathers Estate. Given under our hands this 25th day of July 1713.

Oliver Segar
Robt. Daniell　John Owen (1713)

At a Court held for Middlesex County the 4th day of August 1713
The above account and report is admitted to record

pp.　KNOW ALL MEN by these presents that wee RICE CURTIS and HARRY BEVERLEY
311-　of Middlesex County are bound unto JOHN SMITH Gent first in Comission of the
312　peace for above County in sum of two hundred pounds Sterl. this 1st day of September 1713.

The Condition of this obligation is such that if Rice Curtis Administrator of all the goods and credits of ALLEN FARGUSON deceased doe make a true inventory of all the Estate and render a true account to the Court when requested and if it shall hereafter appear that any last Will and Testamt. was made by the said Deced and the Execor. named doe exhibite the same to said Court and approved said Rice Curtis being thereunto required doe deliver up his Letters of Administration that then this obligation to be voyd otherwise to remaine

In presence of JNO. CURTIS,　　　　　　　　　　Rice Curtis
　　　　　　　　　　　　　　　　　　　　　　　　Harry Beverley

At a Court held for Middlesex County the 1st day of September 1713
This Bond was acknowledged in Court by the Subscribers and admitted to record

pp.　KNOW ALL MEN by these presents that wee MARY MEECHAM, JOHN CLARKE and
312-　HENRY GOODLOE are bound unto JOHN SMITH Gent first in Comission of the peace
313　for said County in sum of five thousand pounds Sterl. this seventh day of Aprill 1713.

The Condtion of this obligation is such that if Mary Meacham shall truely pay unto THOMAS BRAME and JAMES Orphans of JOHN BRAME deced all estate to be due to said Orphans as soon as they attain to lawfull age and shall keep the Justices harmless from all trouble about the said Estate that then this obligation to be voyd or else to be and remain

In presence of WIL. STANARD　　　　　　　　Mary ⁄ᴹᴮ Meacham
　　　　　　　　　　　　　　　　　　John Clarke　Henry Goodloe

At a Court held for Middlesex County the 7th day of Aprill 1713
Mary Meacham, John Clarke & Henry Goodloe came into Court and acknowledged their bond which is admitted to record

p.　KNOW ALL MEN by these presents that wee WILLIAM KILPIN and WILLIAM
313　STANARD of Middlesex County are bound unto our Sovereign Lady Anne in the sume of ten thousand pounds of Tobacco this first day of September 1713.

The Condition of the above obligation is such that Whereas William Kilpin hath obtained a Lycence to keep an Ordinary at his house in URBANNA If Therefore said William Kilpin shall constantly provide good cleanly lodgeing and dyett for travellers and Stableage fodder and provender or pastureage for their horses as the seasons require dureing the terme of one whole year from the first day of September and shall not suffer any unlawfull gameing nor on the Sabbath day suffer any to tipple more then necessary that then this obligation to be voyd otherwise to remain

In presence of JNO. CURTIS,　　　　　　　　W. Kilpin
　　　　　　　　　　　　　　　　　　　　　　Wil: Stanard

Acknowledged in Court by the Subscribers the 1st 7ber 1713 & admitted to record.

pp.   JAMES MEACHAM Executor of the Last Will and Testament of JOHN MEACHAM
313-   deced charges the Estate Dr - To paid his bond dated July ye 12th 1711 to Mr. JA:
315   WALKER, paid GARRITT MINOR p Judgmt; pd bill to Mr. LEO: HILL; pd JONATHAN
        JOHNSON an Orphan his Estate amounting to 2456; to Judgment to WM. STANARD,
to SARAH ONEAL p Judgment; to ALEX. GRAVES p Judgment; pd G. CORBIN; pd JOANNA
BRAME; pd JOHN HORD; pd HENRY JONES; pd NICHOL BRAME; to RICHINS BRAME; to JANE
TAYLOR; to MATTHEW PERRY; to RICHD. ATTWOOD; to JOANNA BRAME; to Mr. SEGAR Sher.
fees; to funerall expences; to one barrell corne lent him in his lifetime
   Contra - By the whole inventory and appraismt. of the Estate of the said deced
amounting to the sum of L 116:15:4; by a set of wedges; by the Cropp; by HENRY JONES;
by WM. STANARD; by JNO. ALDIN; by JOANNA BRAME; by EDWD. CLARKE; by H. JONES
     Errors Excepted this 31st July 1713 p James Meacham Exer of John Meacham deced
   At a Court held for Middx. County the 1st day of September 1713
James Meacham Executor of John Meacham deced produced this account of the deceds
Estate which at his motion is admitted to record

pp.   THIS INDENTURE made the twenty fourth day of August 1713 & in the twelfth
315-   year of the Reigne of our Sovereign Lady Anne Between WILLIAM CARTER of
316   ESSEX COUNTY of one part and JOHN CARTER of Middx. County Witnesseth that for
        sum of Eightene hundred pounds of good sweet scented Tobacco & Caske paid sd
Will: Carter hath by these presents granted unto John Carter forty acres of land in
Middx. County bounded beginning at THO: HEDGCOCKs line upon the rouling path thence
bounding upon sd Hedgcocks line to the line of RICE JONES thence bounding upon sd
Jones upon the Spring Branch of William Carters deceast
In presence of WILL: DANIELL,   William /M\ Carter
     JOHN BRISTOW
   At a Court held for Middx. County the 1st day of September 1713
William Carter came into Court & acknowledged this Deed to John Carter which is ad-
mitted to record DOREAS also the Wife of said William appeared in Court & relinquished
her right of Dower which is hereby certyfied
   KNOW ALL MEN by these presents that I William Carter am bound unto John Carter in
the sume of five thousand pounds of good sweet scented Tobacco & Caske this 24th day of
August 1713. The Condition of this Obligation is such that if William Carter truely ob-
serve all things mentioned in Indenture according to the true meaning that then this
obligation to be voyd or else to stand
   In presence of WILL: DANIELL,   William /M\ Carter
     JOHN BRISTOW
   At a Court held for Middx. County the 1st day of September 1713
William Carter acknowledged this bond to John Carter which is admitted to record

p.   I WILLIAM STANARD Clerk of Middlesex County (being unable at present to at-
317   tend the said Court) to the end the business be not delayed have thought fitt to
        depute and appoint my Kinsman RICHARD HICKMAN of whose ability I doubt not
to officiate for me in all things relateing to the office of Clerk of the said County Court
dureing this present session (desireing the Worshipfull the Justices of the said Court to
admitt him after his takeing the usuall oaths accordingly). Given under my hand and
Seale this third day of November 1713.
                                             WIL. STANARD
   At a Court held for Middlesex County the 3d day of November 1713
This Deputation from Mr. William Stanard Clerk of Middlesex County to Richard

Hickman was ordered to be recorded.

Test R. Hickman D. Cl Cur

pp.   KNOW ALL MEN by these presents that wee EDWD. MOOR, MARGT. MOOR, CHARLES
317-   LEE and ROBERT GEORGE of Middx. County are bound unto MATTHEW KEMP Gent
318   first in the Comission of the peace for the above County in the sum of Fifty
        pounds Sterling this 2d day of February 1713.
    The Condition of this obligation is such that if Edwd. More & Margt. his Wife (Adminis-
trators of the goods & credits of the said WM. SYMONS deced) doe make a perfect Inventory of all the goods and truely administer according to Law and make a just account of
their actings and doings when required and if it shall hereafter appear that any last
Will and Testament was made by said deced Execur. therein named doe exhibit the same
in said Court requesting to have it approved if sd Edwd. Moore being thereunto required
doe deliver up his Letters of Administration that then this obligation to be void otherwise to remain in force
In presence of WM. M CARTER,   Edwd. E Moore Margrett I L Moor
        WM. STANARD   Robert R George Charr. Lee
    Acknowledged in Court by the Subscribers & admitted to record this 2d day of February
1713

pp.   THIS INDENTURE made the nine and twentieth day and the thirtieth day of Janu-
318-   ary 1713 Betweene JOHN SMYTH of Christ Church Parish in County of Middx. of
321   one part and THOMAS BLAKEY of Parish and County aforesaid Witnesseth that
        said John Smyth for the sum of Three thousand pounds of good swt. scented
tobacco and caske hath sold unto said Thomas Blakey in his actuall possession now by
virtue of bargaine and sale and by force of Statute for transferring uses into possession
fifty acres of land in the Parish and County aforesaid bounded beginning att a white
oake standing by the TOWN PATH runing thence North East to the mouth of the GOOD-
LAND SWAMP thence up the Goodland Swamp to a line of JAMAICA LAND thence by a
straight line to the beginning place not trespassing on the Jamaica Land
In presence of JOHN OWEN (1713),   J. Smith
        THOMAS BUFORD; HENRY BUFORD
    At a Court held for Middx. County the 2d day of February 1713
John Smith came into Court & acknowledged his Lease and Release unto Thomas Blakey
which is admitted to record
    KNOW ALL MEN by these presents that I John Smyth am bound unto Thomas Blakey in
sum of six thousand pounds of good sweet scented Tobacco & Caske this thirtieth day of
January 1713.
    The Condition of this obligation is such that if John Smyth shall fullfill all the Cove-
nants mentioned in Indenture that then this obligation to be void otherwise to stand
In presence of JOHN OWEN (1713)   J. Smith
        THOMAS BUFORD, HENRY BUFORD
    At a Court held for Middlesex County the 2d day of February 1713
John Smith acknowledged this bond to Thomas Blakey which is admitted to record

pp.   KNOW ALL MEN by these presents that I CUTHBERT POTTER of the County of LAN-
321-   CASTR: Mercht. for a valuable sume paid by ALEXANDER SMITH of aforesd County
322   before the delivery hereof have sold unto said Alexr. Smith a parcell of land
        containing Seven hundred acres in the County of Lancaster upon the great
Swamp begining at a marked white oake standing by MATTAPONY PATH near the Plan-
tacon of JNO. SMITH and extending it self for bredth from the white oake North West
and by West alongst butting Mattapony Path the due bounds of the Seven hundred acres

of land and extending it selfe its length from the first mentioned white oake down to
the Great Swamp side by a line of marked trees that divides this land and the land of Jo:
Smith To Hold the said Seven hundred acres of land In Consideration whereof I have
sett my hand and Seale this 8th day of March 1665.
In presence of RICHD. JOHNSON,   Cuthbert Potter
      WM. GORDENER
Recognit Com Lancastr 11 die July 1666 record 20th die Sequene
                                          T EDMD. DALE Cl Cur
Vera Copia et Examt. p JOS. TAYLOE CC
At a Court held for Middlesex County the 2d day of February 1713
At the motion of John Smyth this copy of a Deed made by Cuthbert Potter to Alexander
Smith is admitted to record

p.   KNOW ALL MEN by these presents that wee JOHN SMITH, WILLIAM LAWSON and
322   RICE CURTIS are bound unto MATTHEW KEMP Gent first in Comission of the peace
        for said County in sume of Three hundred pounds Sterl. this 2d day of Febry 1713
The Condition of this obligation is such that if John Smith do pay unto SAMUELL SMITH
Orphan of JOHN SMITH deced all such estate as shall appear to be due said Orphan as
soon as he attain to lawfull age and keep harmless said Justices from troubles about the
Estate that then this obligation to be voyd otherwise to remaine
In presence of JNO. CURTIS,   J. Smith
      WIL. STANARD   William Lawson   R. Curtis
   Acknowledged in open Court held for Middx. County the 2d of February 1713 by the
Subscribers to it and admitted to record

pp.   THIS INDENTURE made this first and second day of February in the year 1713
322-   betweene THOMAS MOUNTAGUE Son of PETER MOUNTAGUE of the Parish of Christ
324   Church in County of Middx. of one part & RICE CURTIS of same Parish and County
        Planter Witnesseth that for sum of Sixty pounds Sterl. the said Thomas Mounta-
gue hath granted unto said Rice Curtis in his actuall possession now being by virtue of
a bargain and Sale and by force of the Statute for transferring uses into possession and
to his heirs all that parcell of land containing One hundred and eighteen acres of land
being in the Parrish of Christ Church in County of Middlesex and bounded begining at
a Chesnutt oak standing on the side of a Hill being one of the line trees that parted the
land of PETER MOUNTAGUE SENR. and WILLIAM MOUNTAGUE SENR. and running thence
South East to an Ash tree standing in the fork of the Causey Swamp thence North East to
the mouth of the said Branch to a markt Maple standing in the mouth of the aforesd
Swamp near the Island Marsh thence cross the said Marsh from the PATH that leads to
CURTIS's House from thence up the said branch North to a Dogwood tree standing on the
head of the said Branch thence North Easterly to ye river side thence West Southerly
along the said river side to a markt hickory being a corner tree of the dividing line
between the aforesd two Mountagues and from thence Westerly to the beginning To
Hold the said land unto sd Rice Curtis and his heires
In presence of us HARRY BEVERLEY,   Tho: Mountague Junr.
      J. SMITH, JOHN SEGAR
   At a Court held for Middlesex County the second day of February 1713
Thomas Mountague came this day into Court and acknowledged this Deed of lease and
release to Rice Curtis which is admitted to record

pp.   THIS INDENTURE made this fifth and sixth day of October 1713 Between DANIELL
324-   TRIGG of the Parish of Christ Church in County of Middlesex of one part and

326   ABRAHAM TRIGG of same Parish and County Witnesseth that for sume of Two
        thousand pounds of Tobacco paid by said Abraham Trigg said Daniell Trigg doth
sell unto said Abraham Trigg (his Son) in his actuall possession now being by virtue of
a bargain and sale to him made for one whole year and by force of the Statute for transferring uses into possession a tract of land in this County formerly conveyed by JOHN
WILLIS to EDWARD DOCKER by Deed dated the 12th of November 1683 and by said Edward
Docker sold unto Daniel Trigg and NICHOLAS FOWLES as by an Assignment dated the 8th
day of February 1685/6 and by said Deed and Assignment on records of Middlesex
County Court
In presence of us JNO. CURTIS,   Daniell ⊤ Trigg
      RALPH BAKER, THO: KID; WIL: STANARD
    At a Court held for Middlesex County the 5th day of January 1713
Daniel Trigg acknowledged this his lease and release for land to his Son Abraham Trigg
which is admitted to record.

pp.   THIS INDENTURE made this Eight and Nineth day of February 1713 Between WIL-
326-   LIAM and FRANCIS SANDEFORDs of the Parish of Christ Church in the County of
327   Middlesex of one part and JOHN BRADLEY of the same Parish and County Witnes-
        seth that for sum of Ten thousand pounds of sweet scented Tobo to said William
Sandeford and Francis Sandeford his Wife already paid sold unto said John Bradley his
heires forever a plantation & land in the Parish and County aforesd containing One
hundred acres of land now being by vertue of a bargain and sale and by force of the
Statute for transferring uses into possession all the right of them to the said One hun-
dred acres of land being bounded begining at a Gum tree on Hollowing Point Barr and
thence up the Cove to a Pine tree on the mouth of the first branch thence to a great
Pine on the head of the same branch and from thence to a corner pine joyning to
ALLAMANs line thence to Sr. HENR. CHICHELEYs Corner Tree soe bounding upon
RICHARD STEEVENS, Madm. CHURCHHILL & HENR. ARMISTEAD
In presence of REBECCA ✕ HEWES,   William Sandiford
      WILLIAM ᙭ CHANCELOR, JOHN JOHNSON   Francis ✕ Sandiford
    At a Court held for Middlesex County the 2d day of March 1713
William Sandiford and Francis his Wife came into Court and acknowledged this their
lease and release to John Bradley (the sd Francis being first privately examined) which
is admitted to record

pp.   THIS INDENTURE made the first and second day of February 1713 Between
328-   RICHARD STEEVENS of Parish of Christ Church in County of Middlesex of one
329   part and JOHN JOHNSON of same Parish and County SCHOOLMASTER Witnesseth
        that out of the Brotherly love and affection which he beareth unto said John
Johnson as marrying his Sister ANNE STEEVENS and more particularly for sume of ten
pounds Sterl. money of England by these presents hath sold unto said John Johnson his
heires forever all that plantation and land thereto adjoyning (whereon the said John
Johnson now dwelleth) One hundred acres of land in the actuall possession of said John
Johnson by Virtue of a bargaine and sale and by force of the Statute for transferring
uses into possession all the interest whatsoever said Richard Steevens to said One hundred acres of land bounded begining at the narrows of Stone Point and soe running up
to the first branch beyond the said Johnsons House on the North side of an Old Feild
called SHEPERDs GROUND and along to the head of the said branch and from thence
streight across to my line tree binding upon ADAM CURTIS
In presence of us EDWARD WALFORD,   Richard Steevens
      JONATHAN HERRING, ANNA Ⱥ HERRING

At a Court held for Middlesex County the 2d day of March 1713
Richard Steevens came into Court & acknowledged this his lease and release for land to
John Johnson which is admitted to record

pp.   KNOW ALL MEN by these presents that wee WM. LAWSON & JOHN VIVION of
329-   County of Middlesex are bound unto MATTHEW KEMP gent first in Commission of
330   the peace for said County in sum of Two hundred pounds Sterl. money of Eng-
         land this 6th day of Aprill 1714.
The Condition of this obligation is such that if Wm. Lawson Administrator of all the
goods chattles & credits of JANE LAWSON deced do make a true inventory of all goods of
said deced and farther doe make a just and true account of his actings and doings therein when required and if it shall hereafter appear that any Last Will and Testament was
made by the said deced that said William Lawson as required doe render and deliver up
his Letters of Admon. that then this obligation to be voyd otherwise to remaine
In presence of us JNO. CURTIS,   William Lawson
         THOMAS MOUNTAGUE   Jno. Vivion
    Acknowledged in Court the 6th day of Aprill 1714 & admitted to record

p.   I the Subscriber doe hereby authorise Mr. WM. STANARD my Lawfull Attorney
330   for me to acknowledge in Middlesex County Court my relinquishment of Dower
         of one Lott or halfe acre of land and house in the Town of URBANNA in the
County aforesd. Witness my hand & seale this 5th day of Aprill 1714.
In presence of ROBT. DUDLEY,   AVORILLAH *a* CURTIS
         THO: T DUDLEY
    At a Court held for Middlesex County the 6th day of Aprill 1714
This Letter of Attorney was proved by the oathes of the Witnesses and admitted to record

pp.   THIS INDENTURE made this second day of Aprill 1714 Between JNO. CURTIS of
330-   the County of Middlesex of one part and CHRISTOPHER ROBINSON and JOHN
331   ROBINSON of same County Witnesseth that said John Curtis for sum of four thou-
         sand pounds of Tobacco doth sell unto said Christopher & John Robinson their
heires forever one lott or halfe acre of land with the house thereon in Town of URBAN-
NA lately in the occupation of the said John Curtis but now in occupation of said Christopher and John Robinson
In presence of us WIL. STANARD   Jno. Curtis
         WILLIAM LAWSON
    At a Court held for Middlesex County the 6th day of Aprill 1714
John Curtis came this day into Court and acknowledged the within Deed which is ad-
mitted to record. William Stanard Attorney for AVERILLA CURTIS the Wife of said John
Curtis this day appeared in Court and relinquished all the said Averilla her claime of
Dower in the land which is hereby certified.

p.   KNOW ALL MEN by these presents that wee WILLIAM DANIELL & JOHN BRISTOW
332   of County of Middlesex are bound unto MATTHEW KEMP Gent First in Commission
         of the peace for said County in sum of Fifty pounds sterling money of Great Brit-
tain this 6th day of April 1714.
    The Condition of this obligation is such that if William Daniell (Administrator of all
the goods and credits of MARY DAVIS deced) do make a perfect Inventory of all the
goods and credits of sd deced & exhibit the same into the County Court of Middlesex
when required and make a true acct. of his actings and doings therein when required
and if it shall hereafter appear that any last Will and Testament was made by the sd

deced and the Executors exhibit same in said Court if said Wm. Daniell being required
doe render and deliver up his Letters of Administration that then this obligation to be
voyd otherwise to stand
In presence of JOHN WORMELEY,   Will: Daniell
         WIL: STANARD   John Bristow
    Acknowledged in Court ye 6th of Aprill 1714 & admitted to record

pp.   KNOW ALL MEN by these presents that wee JACOB PRESSON, EDMD. CAMBRIDGE
332-   and HENRY FREEMAN of Middx. County are bound unto MATTHEW KEMP gent
333   first in the Commission of the peace in the sum of Fifty pounds Sterl. money of
         Britaine this 6th day of Aprill 1714
The Condition of this obligation is such that if Jacob Presson (Administrator of all the
goods & credits of THO: WOOD deced) doe make a perfect inventory of all the goods of the
said deced & exhibite the same into sd County Court of Middlesex when required and further do make a true and just account of his actings and doings therein when required
by said Court and if it shall hereafter appear that any last Will and Testament was made
by the said deced and the Exers. therein named doe exhibit the same into Court accordingly if said Jacob Presson deliver up his Letter of Administration then this obligation
to be void otherwise to remaine
In presence of us ZACH: LEWIS,   Jacob Presson
         WM. STANARD   Edmd. 𝒴 Cambridge Henry |⊣ Freeman
    Acknowledged in Court the 6th day of Aprill 1714 & admitted to record

pp.   KNOW ALL MEN by these presents that I FRANCIS WEEKES SENR. of Christ Church
333-   Parish in County of Middlesex Gent have for two hundred & ten pounds Sterling
334   . money to me paid by my Son HOBBS WEEKES of the Parish and County aforesaid
         sould unto my said Sonn Hobbs Weekes three Negroe men slaves Vizt. Bristow,
Ben and Will twenty five head of Cattle, Eleaven sheep and four feather bedds and fur-
niture To Hold unto the abovesaid Hobbs Weekes his heires forever Provided that if said
Francis Weekes shall truely pay unto said Hobbs Weekes the aforesaid sum within the
time of Seven years that then this present Writeting to be void otherwise to stand. In
Witness I have put my hand and seale this 5th day of January 1714/3.
Test   HUMPHRY JONES,   Francis Weekes
         JOHN CHEADLE, PAUL THILMAN
    At a Court held for Middlesex County the 5th day of Janaury 1713
Humphry Jones made oath in Court that he saw Francis Weekes sign the within Deed as
his act and deed which is hereby Certyfied
    At a Court held for Middx. County the 4th day of May 1714
Francis Weekes Senr. came this day into Court and acknowledged this Deed to his Sonn
Hobbs Weekes which is admitted to record
    KNOW ALL MEN by these presents that I Francis Weekes Senr. of the Parish of Christ
Church in Middlesex County gentl. doe owe unto Hobbs Weekes the sum of Four hun-
dred and twenty pounds Sterl. money this Fifth day of January 1713.
    The Condition of this obligation is such that if Francis Weekes Senr. shall well and
truely pay the full sum of two hundred and tenn pounds Sterling money within seaven
yeares that then this obligation to be void otherwise to stand
In presence of us HUMPHRY JONES,   Francis Weekes
         JOHN CHEADLE, PAUL THILMAN
    At a Court held for Middlesex County the 5th day of January 1713
Humphry Jones made Oath he saw Francis Weekes sign the above bond which is hereby
certified

At a Court held for Middx. County the 4th day of May 1714
Francis Weekes came into Court and acknowledged the above bond & it is admitted to record.

pp.
335-
336

THIS INDENTURE made the first day of June 1714 Between RICE JONES of Middlesex County Planter of one part and SUSANA ROBINSON late Widow of THOMAS MRITHER of ESSEX COUNTY Gentl. deced and SUSANA MERIWEATHER Daughter of the said Thomas Merriweather on the other part Witnesseth that whereas said Thomas Meriwether in his lifetime in the year 1706 did agree with said Rice Jones for the Old Mill and Dam called COXES MILLS then formerly belonging to MAURICE COCK deced and two acres and a half of land thereto adjoyning in Middlesex County beginning at a red oake standing by the Mill Pond and thence running North East to a Mulberry tree thence East on the brow of a Hill to a line that divides this land from the land of GARRETT MINOR and so along that line crossing the swamp to the place it began one acre whereof is that acre of land which said Rice Jones purchased of GAWIN CORBIN Esqr. and the other acre & halfe is that which lies on the South side of ye dam and is excepted by the said Rice Jones in his Deed of sale to Garrett Minor according as it is bounded by marked trees made by the said Rice Jones and Garrett Minor and the said Thomas Meriwether did then in full consideration sell to sd Rice Jones one negro man slave of ye value of fifty pounds Sterl. and did thereupon proceed to renew & repair the said Dam and built a new water mill thereon and hath continued in possession of the same from the said time to ye day of his death and the said Susana his relict and Susanna his Daughter according to the Will of said Thomas to this present time and are still in possession but never had a firm Deed of Sale from the said Rice Jone for the same and whereas the said Rice Jones after the bargain made with the said Thomas Meriwether and the sd Negro Slave reced Viz. the Sixth day of January 1706 at the Parish of Southfarnham in County of Essex did give bond to sd Thomas in sum of Three hundred pounds of lawfull money of England with condition (in case of said Thomas his death before conveyance made) to make a good conveyance of same to such person as said Thomas should dispose of the same to by Will according to the directions of his Will Now the said Rice Jones being fully in compliance with his said bond and in pursuance of the Will of said Thomas Meriwether hath for himselfe & his heires sold unto the said Susana Robinson one third part of the said Water Mill for and dureing her naturall life and the other two third parts of the said Mill to the said Susanna the Daughter of the said Thomas and after the death of the said Susanna the whole Mill and Land aforesd to the said Susanna the Daughter and to the heirs of her body lawfully begotten and in default of such heires then to WILLIAM MERIWETHER, DAVID MERIWETHER and NICHOLAS MERIWETHER Sons of Majr. NICHOLAS MERIWETHER Brother to the said Thomas Meriwether and to their heires forever equally to be divided according to the meaning of said Will

In presence of us GEORGE WORTHAM,   Rice Jones
        JNO. VIVION

At a Court held for Middlesex County the first day of June 1714
Rice Jones came into Court and acknowledged the within Deed to be his act and deed which is admitted to record.

pp.
336-
337

KNOW ALL MEN by these presents that wee THOMAS MOUNTAGUE and GARRETT MINOR of Middx. County are bound unto MATTHEW KEMP Gent first in Comission of the peace for above County in sum of Five hundred pounds Sterl. this first day of June 1714.

The Condition of this obligation is such that if Thos. Mountague Exer. of the last Will

and Testament of WM. MOUNTAGUE deced do make a true and perfect inventory of all the goods and credits of the said deced and further doe make a true and just Acct. of his actings and doings therein when required and truely pay the Legacys contained in the said Testamt. that then this obligation to be void otherwise to remaine in force
In presence of ROBT. PERROTT,   Thomas Mountague
                                                  Garritt Minor
    At a Court held for Middx. County the first day of June 1714
This bond acknowledged in Court and admitted to record

p.   KNOW ALL MEN by these presents that wee ELIZABETH FOSTER and JOHN HIP-
337   KINGS of Middx. County are bound unto MATTHEW KEMP Gentl. first in Comission
        of the peace for said County in sum of two hundred pounds Sterl. this first day of
June 1714. The Condition of this obligation is such that if Elizabeth Foster (Administra-trix of all the goods and credits of JOHN FOSTER deced) do make a true inventory of all the goods and credits of the said deced and exhibit the same in the County Court of Middx. as required and further do make a true account of her actings and doings there-in when required and deliver unto such persons as the said Justices by their Order shall direct and if it shall hereafter appear that any last Will and Testament was made by said deced and the Exer. doe exhibite the same in said Court if said Eliza. doe render up her Letter of Approbation of such Testament being first had in said Court that then this obligation to be voyd otherwise to remain
In presence of us THOS: HENMEN,   Elizabeth & Foster
    WIL. STANARD ClCur   John Hipkings
    At a Court held for Middlesex County the first day of June 1714
This bond acknowledged in Court & admitted to record

p.   KNOW ALL MEN by these presents that I AMBROSE BURFOOT SENR. of Lyn Haven
338   Parrish and PRINCESS ANNE COUNTY in the Government of Virginia have made
        my well beloved friend ROBERT DUDLEY my true and lawfull Attorney in my
place upon one certain parcell of land being One hundred and fifty acres of land in Middlesex County in the Government of Virginia which by THOMAS DUDLEY and WIL-LIM ELLIOTT of said County of Middlesex was out of a greater Patent of land comonly called the Green Branch to me the said Ambrose Barfoote sould to take the same in pos-session and to sell and convey I do promise to hold firme & stable whatsoever my said Attorney shall doe. In Witness I have set my hand and Seale this tenth day of March 1713/14.
In presence of THOS: T DUDLEY,   Ambross X Burfoot
    THOS. R ROBINSON; WILLIAM M DANLO,
    MARY C CUFFELY
    At a Court held for Middx. County the first day of June 1714
The Within Letter of Attorney was this day proved in Court by the oaths of Thos. Dudley and Thos: Robinson & admitted to record.

pp.   KNOW ALL MEN by these presents that wee CHARLES COOPER, WM. GARDNER and
338-   JNO. HARDEE of Middx. County are bound unto MATTHEW KEMP Gent. first in the
339   Comission of the peace for said County in sum of Fifty pounds Sterl. this first day
        of June 1714.
The Condition of this obligation is such that if Charles Cooper (Administrator of all the goods and credits of JOHN BONE deced) doe make a perfect inventory of all the said Es-tate & cause to be exhibited in the Court of Middlesex County and further doe make a just and true account of his actings and doings therein when required and if it shall hap-

pen that any last Will and Testament was made by the said deced and Exers. named do exhibit the same in Court if Charles Cooper being required doe deliver up his Letrs of
Admon. in said Court that then this obligation to be voyd otherwise to remaine

In presence of us JNO. CURTIS,   Charles Cooper

                                       Wm. Gardner   Jno. Hardee

At a Court held for Middx. County the first day of June 1714
This Bond was acknowleged in Court & admitted to record

p.   KNOW ALL MEN by these presents that wee JOHN VIVION, WILLIAM STANARD &
339   JOHN SEGAR of County of Middlesex are bound unto our Sovereign Lady Anne in
       sum of one thousand pounds Sterl. this sixth day of July 1714.

The Condition ofthe above obligation is such that Whereas John Vivion is by Commission under the hand of the Honble. the Lt. Governor ALEXANDER SPOTSWOOD bearing
date the 28th Aprill 1714 appointed Sheriff of the abovesaid County of Middx. if therefore the above bound John Vivion doe well and truely render unto Mr. Auditor LUD-
WELL a just account of all her Majts. Revenues in said County dureing the time of his
Sherivalty and payment make of all such publick dues as shall be levyed and also to
faithfully performe his Office of Sheriff that then the above obligation to be voyd and
otherwise to stand

In presence of JNO. CURTIS,   John Vivion

      JNO. THACKER   Wil. Stanard   John Segar

Acknowledged in open Court held for Middx. County the 6th day of July 1714 by the
Subscribers to it & admitted to record

pp.   THIS INDENTURE made the 2d and third day of August 1714 Between ROBERT DUD-
340- LEY of County of Middlesex of one part and JOHN MAYO of the same County
343   WHEREAS said Robert Dudley by Indenture dated the 2d day of August did sell
       unto said John Mayo One hundred acres of land in the Parish of Christ Church
in County of Middlesex being part of a tract formerly belonging to said ROBT. DUDLEY
Father and now in possession of ye said John Mayo being bounded begining at a Corner
Hickory tree standing on the mouth of a small branch by the side of the Great Swamp
called Bobs Swamp and runing along the small branch keeping its naturall bounds
thence Southwest to two corner Hickorys standing by Mr. HENRY ARMISTEADs line
thence along said Armisteads line to a white oak standing in the aforesd Bobs Swamp up
the said Swamp to the first begining place To Hold the said land unto John Mayo to the
intent that by virtue of the Statute for transferring uses into possession the said John
Mayo might be in actuall possession of said lands NOW THIS INDENTURE WITNESSETH
that said Robert Dudley for sum of Fourty four pounds Sterling money of England hath
sold unto John May the said land

In presents of JNO. VIVION,   Robt. Dudley

     JOHN DAVIS, JNO. CURTIS

At a Court held for Middlesex County the 3d day of August 1714
Robert Dudley came into Court and acknowledged the lease and release of land to John
Mayo which is admitted to record ELIZABETH also the Wife of said Robert Dudley ap-
peared in open Court and relinquished her right of Dower which is hereby certifyed

KNOW ALL MEN by these presents that I Robert Dudley am bound unto John Mayo in
sum of Two hundred pounds Sterling money of England this 3d day of August 1714

The Condition of this obligation is such that if Robert Dudley shall truely keep all the
Covenants mentioned in certain lease and release to John Mayo that then this obligation to be void otherwise to remain

In presents of JNO VIVION,   Robt. Dudley
     JOHN DAVIS, JOSEPH Ɨ ALPHIN
At a Court held for Middlesex County the 3d day of August 1714
Robert Dudley came into Court & acknoweldged this bond which is admitted to record

pp.   THIS INDENTURE made the second and third day of August 1714 Between ROBERT
343-   DUDLEY of County of Middlesex of one part and JOHN DAVIS of same WHEREAS
345   said Robert Dudley by Indenture dated the 3d day of August did sell unto said
John Davis One hundred acres of land in the Parish of Christ Church in County
of Middlesex being part of a tract of land formerly belonging to said Robert Dudleys
Father and now in possession of said John Davis being bounded as followeth begining at
a marked white oak standing on the North East Hill of a small branch commonly called
Sandey Branch and runing thence Southwest along a line of marked trees until it meets
with Mr. HENRY ARMISTEADs land formerly called KIBLES line to a marked Hickory tree
thence along said Kibles line to another line of said Armisteads formerly called
THACKERS line then along Thackers line to the first beginning place To Hold unto said
John Davis by Virtue of statute for transferring uses into possession that ye said John
Davis might be in actuall possession of said lands Now This Indenture Witnesseth that
said Robert Dudley for sum of Fifteen pounds Sterling money of England and four thou-
sand five hundred pounds of sweet scented Tobacco hath sold unto said John Davis the
aforesaid land
In presents of JNO. VIVION,   Robt. Dudley
     JOHN MAYO, JOSEPH Ɨ ALPHIN   John Davis
At a Court held for Middx. County the 3d day of August 1714
Robert Dudley came into Court and acknowledged the above lease and release to John
Davis which is admitted to record ELIZABETH also Wife of said Robert appeared in open
Court and relinquished her right of Dower in the land which is hereby Certyfied
   KNOW ALL MEN by these presents that I Robert Dudley am bound unto John Davis in
the sum of two hundred pounds Sterling money of England this 3d day of August 1714.
   The Condition of this obligation is such that if Robert Dudley truely perform all
agreements made in Indenture on his part that then this obligation to be void other-
ways to stand
In presents of JNO. VIVION,   Robt. Dudley
     JOHN MAYO
At a Court held for Middx. County the 3d day of August 1714
Robert Dudley came into Court & acknowledged his bond to John Davis which is admitted
to record

p.   KNOW ALL MEN by these presents that wee WILLIAM KILPIN, JNO. VIVION and
346   WILLIAM STANARD are bound unto our Sovereign Lady Anne in sum of ten
       thousand pounds of Tobo this 3d day of August 1714.
   The Condition of this obligation is such that Whereas William Kilpin hath obtained a
Lycence to keep an ORDINARY at his House in URBANNA if said Wm. Kilpin doth provide
good and cleanly lodging and dyett for travellers and Stableage fodder and provender
or pasturage for their horses as the seasons require and dureing the terme of one
whole year from 3d day of August 1714 and shall not permitt any unlawfull gameing or
on the Sabbath day suffer any to tipple more than is necessary that then this obligation to be void otherwise to remaine
In presence of JNO. THACKER,   W. Kilpin
                                      Jno. Vivion   Wm. Stanard
Acknowledged in Court held for Middlesex County ye 3d August 1714.

p.   Reced of Mrs. ELIZABETH CHURCHHILL & RALPH WORMELEY Exers. of WM.
346   CHURCHHILL Esqr. deceased the sum of one hundred pounds Sterl. and the Sum
       of twenty five pounds in goods reasonably rated for Acct of my two Children by
named SUSANNA and CHURCHHILL JONES the said Sums being left as Legacies to the said
Susanna and Churchhill Jones by Will of WILLIAM CHURCHHILL Esqr. deceased. As
Witness my hand this 4th day of November 1713.
Wittness JNO. LOMAX   ROGR. JONES
   At a Court held for Middx. County the 3d day of August 1714
At motion of Mrs. Elizabeth Churchhill the above receipt is admitted to record.

p.   At a Court held for Middlesex County the 4th day of May 1714
346   The Attachment which JOHN DEGGE obtained against WILLIAM DEAKERs Estate
       for his non appearance at the Suit of JONATHAN HERRING being returned served
on Looking Glass, Kersey Coat, one druget Waisecoat & britches, seven Ells of Sheeting
holland, five Ells 3/4 of Dowelg. one small trunck, one Dowlas shirt, one chest, one pair
of old tick britches. It is ordered that ye Sheriff cause the said attached particulars to
be appraised according to Law and that he deliver them to the Plt and report his proceedings to ye next Court.
   Pursuant to ye within Ordr. wee the Subscribers being first sworn have valued the following goods - Total 600 lb
May ye 31 1714   THO: MACHEN   GEORGE BERRICK
                   PETER P BRUMMENILL   JACOB STIFFE
   At a Court held for Middx.County the 3d day of August 1714
The within Order & apprment are admitted to record

p.   At a Court held for Middlesex County the 4th day of May 1714
347   In an Action of Debt between WILLIAM BLACKBURNE Plt and WM. DEAKER Deft.
       wherein there was an attachment granted which attachmt. being returned exe-
cuted on the Kersey Coat unlined, Six Ells of Garlick holland & pr of worsted hose, 3 ells
of brown linnen, check shirt & check handkerchiefs It is ordered that the Sheriff
cause the said particulars to be appraised and delivered to the Plt and report his proceedings in the next Court
   Pursuant to the within order we the Subscribers being first sworn according to Law
have valued and appraised the following Goods Total 344 1/4   May 31st 1714
                   THO: MACHEN   GEO: BERRICK
                   PETER P BRUMMELL   JACOB STIFFE
   At a Court held for Middx. County the 4th day of August 1714
The Within order & apprmt. are admitted to record

pp.   At a Court continued and held for Middlesex County the 4th day of August 1714
347-   Mr. HARRY BEVERLEY Attorney for ANNE GODDINS moeving this Court that her
348   account against THOMAS GARDNERs Estate may be allowed her Mr. JOHN GRYMES
       and Mr. JOHN VIVION are hereby appointed and desired some time between this
and the next Court to settle the Accounts between Anne Goddin the Widow of THOMAS
GODDIN deced and Thomas Gardiner and returne their proceedings to the next Court.
   Dr. 1710. The Estate of Thomas Gardner deced.
   To Anne Goddin Relict of Thos: Goddin deced - An acct. she produced against said Estate
written by NATHAN UNDERWOOD and signed by Tho: Godin dated 1710. Money paid
Madm. CHURCHHILL, To MARY GIBBS, to MARGARITT WHITLOCK, to WM. MATHERS, to
DOCTER CRANOVATE, to DOCTER WALFORD, to WM. NUBERRY, to DIANA UNDERWOOD, To
funeral charges for Gardener and his Wife

Contra - by Goods not delivered, 1 horse, 1 pr mens falls, parcell of old Iron, 1 Bushell of Salt, by six year old Stear Total 34..9..10.

We the Subscribers in Obedience to an Order of Middlesex County Court dated the 4th day of August 1714 have mett and settled the Account according to the aforesaid Order and doe find the ballance due to Ann Goddin the sum of twenty pounds Six shillings and Seven pence settled this 4th day of September 1714.

                                    JOHN GRYMES   JNO. VIVION
At a Court held for Middx. County the 7th day of September 1714
This Account and report are admitted to record

p.   KNOW ALL MEN by these presents that wee ANNE GODDIN & HARRY BEVERLEY of
348   Middlesex County are bound unto MATTHEW KEMP Gent. first in Commission of
        the peace for said County in sum of one hundred pounds Sterl. this 7th day of
September 1714.

The Condition of this obligation is such that if Anne Goddin Administratrix with the Will annexed of all the goods and credits of THOMAS GODDIN deced doe make a true inventory and exhibit at ye County Court and doe make return and truly administer the same according to law that then this obligation to be void otherwise to remaine
In presence of JNO. CURTIS,   Ann   Goddins
    WM. STANARD   Harry Beverley
At a Court held for Middlesex County the 7th day of September 1714
This bond was acknowledged by the Subscribers to it and admitted to record

p.   KNOW ALL MEN by these presents that wee EDWARD PENDERGRASS and WILLIAM
349   WOOD are bound unto MATTHEW KEMP Gent first in Commission of the peace for
        the County of Middlesex in sum of thirty pounds Ster. this 7th day of September
1714. The Condition of this obligation is such that if Edward Pendergrass shall truely pay unto JOHN HICKEY & CHARLES HICKEY Orphans of JOHN HICKEY deced all Estate as due to sd Orphans as soon as they attain lawfull age and keep harmless said Justices from all troubles about the Estate that then this obliglation to be voyd otherwise to be
In presence of us THO: SMITH,   Edw. Pendergrass
    WM. STANARD   Wm. W Wood
At a Court held for Middx. County the 7th day of September 1714
This Bond was acknowledged in Court by the subscribers to it and admitted to record

pp.   At a Court held for Middx. County the 3d day of August 1714
349-   Upon ye Petition of JOHN PRICE for land for a MILL it is ordered that JOHN NASH
350   and RICHARD ALLIN lay of an acre of land on ye South side the nearest branch
        of Sunderland Creek in ye most convenient place contiguous to the land said
Price to build a WATER MILL on and that said Price be possessed of the same and it is hereby ordered yt: they report their proceedings to next Court

Middx. SS In pursuance to an order of Court Wee have laid of an acre of land for use of Mr. Jno. Price upon the South side of ye branch of Sunderland Creek upon the land of JOHN WILLIAMS and ANNE his Wife in the most convenient place adjacent to land of said Price to build a Water Mill on bounded thus beginning at a Chincopin Tree standing by the Marsh a little below said Prices Mill Dam thence directly up ye hill & by a line of marked trees to an old feild thence up said old feild to a small chesnut by the Marsh thence down and alongst the edge of the marsh to the beginning which acre of land we have valued to be worth ten shillings and have put said Price in Legall possession of the same this 24th day of August 1714
                    JOHN C NASH   RICHARD ALLIN R A

At a Court held for Middx. County the 7th day of September 1714
At the motion of John Price Gentl. this report is admitted to record

p.   KNOW ALL MEN by these presents that wee MARY ALLFORD and WM. GARDENER
350   of Middx. County are bound unto MATTHEW KEMP Gentl. first in Commission of
      the peace in sum of one hundred pounds this 7th day Septembr: 1714
The condition of this obligation is such that if Mary Alford Administratrix of all the
goods and credits of RICHARD ALLFORD deced doe make a true inventory of said deceased
Estate and further make a true account of her actings and doings therein when required and if it shall appear that any last Will and Testament was made by the said deceased if said Mary Allford deliver up her Letters of Administration that then this obli-
gation to be voyd otherwise to remain
In presence of JNO. CURTIS,   Mary ⸮ Allford
          WM. STANARD   Wm. W Gardner
At a Court held for Middx. County the 7th day of Septembr: 1714
This bond was acknowledged by the subscribers to it and admitted to record

pp.   THIS INDENTURE made this 5th day of October in ye year of our Lord God accor-
351- ding to the Account used in England 1714 between ELEANOR KEMP of County of
353   ESSEX Widow of one part and JOHN ALLDIN of County of Middlesex WHEREAS the
      said Eleanor Kemp by Indentur bearing date the 5th of October in said 1714 for
consideration did sell unto John Alldin Son of said Eleanor Kemp for the love I have to
my said Son in consideration of a bond given by my sade Son John Alldin payable to my
two Daughters in Essex MARY NALLE and CATHERINE TORBETT hath sold unto sade John
Alldin that is to say the land which he now lives on calld by name of BASENIN and all
that land belonging to ye Plantation where my Brother RICHARD WILLIS lived and a
parcell of land which did belong to my Brother Richard Willis lying on the South side
of the White Oak Swamp with its share of ye Dragon Swamp the plantation called the
White Oak Plantation together with all my right of a parcell of land lying between the
Green Branch and the Bryery Swamp being the remainder of a Pattent whereof part
was sold to ABRAHAM WEEKES deceased and all other land wherein I have any right
which sade lands are being in the County of Middlesex and it is agreed upon betwixt the
above said parties that she shall not be hindred from living upon the said plantation
and working with hands she hath with the use of what timber she hath occasion for
and dureing her naturall life and at her decease the said plantation and appurtenances
shall remain with said John Alldin and heirs forever
Witnesses JOS. HARDEE,   Eleanor Kemp
          GARRITT MINOR, JOHN BRISTOW
At a Court held for Middx.County the 5th day of October 1714
Eleanor Kemp came into Court & acknowledged this her lease and release to her Son
John Alldin which is admitted to record
KNOW ALL MEN by these presents that I Eleanor Kemp of ESSEX COUNTY am bound unto
my Son John Alldin of County of Middlesex in sum of one thousand pounds Sterling
money of England this 5th day of October 1714.
The Condition of this obligation is such that if Eleanor Kemp shall keep all things
mentioned in Indenture and shall not lay any clame to the sade lands that then this
bond to be void otherwise to stand
In presents of us JOS. HARDEE   Eleanor Kemp
          GARRITT MINOR, JOHN BRISTOW
At a Court held for Middx. County the 5th day of October 1714
Eleanor Kemp came into Court & acknowledged the bond to John Alldin which is ad-

mitted to record

pp.   THIS INDENTURE maid this fourth and fifth day October 1714 Between RICHARD
353-   PERROTT of County of Middlesex of one part and OLIVER SEGAR of same Whereas
357   Richard Perrott by Indenture the date the day before the date hereof did sell
        unto said Oliver Segar all that Tenement and dwelling house wherein JOSEPH
HARDEE now liveth and parcel of land and plantacons adjoyning containing One hundred and thirty acres of land begining at a Corner Populer of Mr. JAMES MICHAMs
standing in a branch on the lower side of this land running thence up the said branch
and along the line of Mr. JOHN CLARKE and then East near unto a red oak in the Widow
PARROTTs old feild thence East North down a branch called the Flax Pond Branch into
the Marsh and along the creek or gullie in said marsh to a small branch which devides
this land from Mr. JAMES MEACHAMs land thence South to the first beginning To Hold
the said land to the end that by vertue of the Statute for Transferring uses into possession the said Oliver Segar might be in actuall possession Now This Indenture Wittnesseth that the said Richard Parrott for sum of Eight thousand pounds of sweet scented
Tobacco paid doth sell unto said Oliver Segar all the aforesaid tract of land
In presence of GARRITT MINOR,   Richd. Perrott
      WILLIAM W GARDNER, JOHN WATTS
  At a Court held for Middlesex County the 8th day of Octobr: 1714
Richard Perrott came into Court and acknowledged his lease and release to Oliver Segar
which is admitted to record SARAH PERROTT the Wife of said Richard this day appeared
in Court and being first examined relinquished her right of Dower in the land which is
hereby certified.
  KNOW ALL MEN by these presents that I Richard Perrott am bound unto Oliver Segar in
sum of Sixteen thousand pounds of good sweet scented Tobacco this fifth day of October
1714. The Condition of this Obligation is such that if Richard Parrott keep all conditions
mentioned in Indentures of lease and release to Oliver Segar that then this obligation to
be voyd otherwise to stand
In presents of GARRITT MINOR,   Richd. Perrott
      WILLIAM W GARDNER, JOHN WATTS
 At a Court held for Middx. County the 5th day of Octobr: 1714
Richard Perrott came into Court and acknowledged his Bond to Oliver Segar which is
admitted to record

pp.   KNOW ALL MEN by these presents that wee JNO. MILLER and JOHN SANDEFORD
357-   are bound unto JOHN SMITH Gent first in Commission of the peace for the County
358   of Middlesex in the sum of two hundred pounds Sterling this fifth day of October
       1714.
  The Condition of this obligation is such that if John Miller (Administrator of JNO. HILL
deceased) do make a true inventory of said deceased Estate and make a just account of
his actings and doings therein and if it shall appear that any last Will and Testament
was made by said Deced if said John Miller doe deliver up his Letters of Administration
that then this obligation to be void otherwise to remain
In presence of JN. THACKER   Jno. X Miller
                                         John Sandeford
  At a Court held for Middx. County the 5th day of October 1714
The above bond was acknowledged by the Subscribers to it & admitted to record

p.   KNOW ALL MEN by these presents that wee JOHN WORMELEY and CHR. ROBINSON
358   of Middlesex County are bound unto JOHN SMITH Gentl. first in comission of the
        peace for said County in sum of ten thousand pounds Sterl. this 5th day of Octo-
ber 1714. The Condition of this obligation is such that if John Wormeley Execr. of the
last Will and Testament of RALPH WORMELEY deced do make a perfect Inventory of all
the said deceased Estate and truely administer according to Law and make a just account
of his actings and doings therein and deliver all the Legacys that then this obligation
to be void otherwise to remain
In presence of JNO. CURTIS,   Jno. Wormeley
        JN. THACKER   Chr. Robinson
    At a Court held for Middlesex County the 5th day of October 1714
The above bond was acknowledged by the Subscribers to it and admitted to record

p.   KNOW ALL MEN by these presents that wee GEORGE WORTHAM & WILLIAM
359   STANARD of County of Middlesex are bound unto JOHN SMITH Gentl. first in
        comission of the peace for said County in sum of one hundred and fifty pounds
Sterl. this 5th day of October 1714.
    The Condition of this obligation is such that if George Wortham (Administrator of
SARAH WORTHAM deceased) doe make a true inventory of all the goods of the said deceased when required and further doe make a true account of his actings and doings
therein when required and if it shall hereafter appear that any last Will and Testament
was made by said deceased if said George Wortham doe deliver up his letter of Administration that then this obligation to be void otherwise to remain
In presence of JN. THACKER,   George Wortham
                                                      Wil. Stanard
    At a Court held for Middx. County the 5th day of October 1714
The above bond was acknowledged by the Subscribers to it & admitted to record

pp.   KNOW ALL MEN by these presents that wee JOHN BRISTOE, MARY BRISTOE and
359-   JAMES MEACHAM of Middx. County are bound unto JOHN SMITH Gentl. first in
360   Commission of the peace for the abovesd County in sum of two hundred pounds
        Sterl. this 6th day of October 1714.
    The Condition of this obligation is such that if John Bristow and Mary his Wife Execu-
trix of the last Will and Testament of WM. CARTER deced doe make a true inventory of
said deceased Estate and truely administer according to Law and truely pay all the
Legacys that then this obligliation to be void otherwise to remain
In presence of us JNO. CURTIS,   John Bristow
        JN. THACKER   James Meacham
    At a Court contd. & held for Middx. County the 6th day of October 1714
The above bond was acknowledged in Court by the Subscribers to it & admitted to record

p.   KNOW ALL MEN by these presents that I EDWARD WALFORD of Middlesex County
360   for a valuable consideration received being in satisfaction of a Judgment for
        Twelve hundred and eighty three pounds of good sweet scented Tobacco obtained
against me by WILLIAM STANARD doe hereby make over to said William Stanard four
head of Cattle, to hold to him forever. In Witness I have sett my hand and seale this 6th
day of October 1714.
Wittness ZACHARY LEWIS,   Edward Walford
        JAMES HACKNEY
    At a Court continued & held for Middx. County the 6th day of October 1714
Edward Walford came into Court & acknowledged the within Deed to William Stanard

which is admitted to record.

pp.   Sir. Pray record one four year old heffar to JOHN LAWRENCE the Son of EDWARD
360-   LAWRENCE to him and his aires forever I haveing the bull calfes and he the Cow
361   calfes of her and what comes of her till he comes of age which I warrant from
        clame of any parson I do now more save only that I am your Servant to
command whilst I am poore   HENRY BARNES
  At a Court continued and held for Middx. County the 8th day of November 1714
Henry Barnes acknowledged the above to John Lawrence which is admitted to record

p.   KNOW ALL MEN by these presents that wee JOHN ROBINSON & CHRISTOPHER
361   ROBINSON gentl. are bound unto ye Honble. ALEXANDER SPOTSWOOD Esqr. Her
        Majts. Lt. Governour and Commander in Cheif of this Dominion in the penalty of
two thousand pounds lawfull money of Virginia this third day of November 1714.
  Whereas by an Act of Assembly made at her Majestie Queen Annes Royall Capitoll begun at Williamsburgh ye 22d day of October in the 11th year of the Reign of our
Sovereign Lady Anne 1712 and thence continued by severall prorogations to the fifth
day of November 1713 and in the 12th year of her Majts. Reign Entituled an Act for
Preventing Frauds in Tobacco and ye Better Improveing the Staple of Tobacco, it is
provided that Storehouses shall be erected and built wherein all Tobaccoes shall be
viewed and Stamped before any Tobaccoes shall be laden on board any Shipp or Vessell
in order to export such Tobaccoes out of this Colony and that ye Governour or Commander in Cheif shall commissionate and appoint persons accordingly and Whereas the
above bound John Robinson Gentl. hath a Commission from the Honble. Alexander
Spotswood to be Agent of the Store House att URBANNA in Middlesex County Now the
Condition of this obligation is that if John Robinson Gentl. shall in all things relateing
to the Office of an Agent hereafter & fairly demean himself according to the intent and
meaning of the aforesaid Act that then the above obligation to be voyd otherwise to
remain in full force
In presence of us WIL. STANARD   Jno. Robinson
            JN.THACKER   Chrr. Robinson
  At a Court continued and held for Middx. County the 8th day of November 1714
John Robinson and Christopher Robinson gentl. came into Court and acknowledged the
above bond to be their act and deed which is admitted to record.

p.   KNOW ALL MEN by these presents that wee JOHN VIVION & WILLIAM STANARD
362   Gentl. of County of Middlesex doe stand bound unto our Sovereign Lord the King
        in Sum of twenty thousand six hundred and fourteen pounds of Tobacco the 7th
day of December 1714.
  The Condition of this obligation is such that if John Vivion Sheriff shall truely collect
the publick and County Levies and pay unto the respective creditors directed to be paid
by an Act of Assembly at the Generall Assembly begun at her Maties. Queen Anne
Royall Capitoll the 23d day of October 1705 and also one other Act of Assembly the 22d
day of October 1712 and continued to the 4th November 1713 entituled an Act for Preventing fraud in Tobacco payments that then this obligation to be void othewise to
remain in full force
In presence of JN. THACKER   Jno. Vivion
                                                     Wil. Stanard

  At a Court held for Middx. County the 7th day of December 1714
This bond was acknowledged by the Subscribers to it & admitted to record

p.   KNOW ALL MEN by these presents that wee MATTHEW PERRY, RICHARD STEEVENS
362   and THOMAS ELLIOTT are bound unto our Sovereign Lord George in the sum of
        ten thousand pounds of Tobacco the 1st day of Febry. 1714.
   The Condition of this obligation is such that Whereas Matthew Perry hath obtained a
lycence to keep an ORDINARY at the COURT HOUSE if therefore he doth constantly provide cleanly lodging and dyett for travellers and stableage fodder provender or
pastureage for their horses as the seasons require dureing the term of one year from
the first day of Febry and shall not permitt any unlawfull gameing nor on the Sabbath
suffer any to tipple more then is necessary that then this obligation to be void otherwise to remain
In presence of us JN. THACKER,   Mattw. Perry
        WM. STANARD   Richard Steevens   Thomas Elliott
   At a Court held for Middx. County the first day of Febry. 1714
The above bond was presented in Court and acknowledged by the subscribers to it &
admitted to record

p.   KNOW ALL MEN by these presents that wee LETTICE PATEMAN and JOHN JOHNSON
363   are bound unto MATTHEW KEMP Gentl. first in Commission of the peace for the
        County of Middlesex in sum of one hundred pounds Sterl. this 1st day of Febry
1714. The Condition of this oblgiation is such that if Lettice Pateman (Administratrix of
THOMAS PATEMAN deced) do make a true inventory of the said Estate and exhibit the
same in County Court and truely administer according to Law and if it shall hereafter
appear that any last Will and Testament was made by said deced then Lettice Pateman
required to deliver up her letters of Administration that then this obligation to be void
otherwise to remain
In presence of us JN. THACKER,   Lettice ⊤ Pateman
        WM. STANARD   John ╪ Johnson
   At a Court held for Middx. County the first day of Febry 1714
The above bond was acknowledged by the Subscribers to it and admitted to record

pp.   THIS INDENTURE made this 31st day Janry 1714 and the first day of February
363-   1714 Between RALPH LOYALL of County of Middlesex of one part and MATTHEW
366   HUNT of same Wittnesseth that said Ralph Loyall for consideration of one thou-
        sand pounds of sweet scented Tobacco doth sell unto Matthew Hunt a parcell of
land with plantation and houseing and that part of ye Dragon Swamp belonging & containing Sixty acres of land in the Parish of Christ Church the County of Middlesex being
part of a Pattent taken up by old WILLIAM DUDLEY and sold to WM. LOYALL SENR. and
bounded beginning at a Ring Oak standing on the head of a small Valley being the
Eastermost Valley of a small branch comly called Barren Neck Branch running thence
North West to a gum that stands by JOHN BATCHELDERs line thence along the said
Batcheldors line South West to the Dragon Swamp Run thence along said Run keeping
its naturall bounds untill it meets with the run of aforesaid Barron Neck Branch then
up the said Branch to the first beginning To Hold the said land to the intent that by vir-
tue of Statute for transferring uses into possession said land shall be in actuall posses-
sion of Matthew Hunt Now This Indenture Witnesseth that for sum of Six thousand
pounds of sweet scented Tobacco to him paid doth release unto said Matthew Hunt all the
Estate right of said Ralph Loyall in same
In presents of JNO. VIVION,   Ralph ꓩ Loyall
        J. SMITH, JA: CURTIS JUNR.
   At a Court held for Middlesex County the first day of Febry 1714
Ralph Loyall this day came into Court and acknowledged his lease and release for land

to Matthew Hunt which is admitted to record AMEY also the Wife of said Ralph appeared in open Court and relinquished her right of Dower which is hereby Certyfied

pp. 367- 368   THIS INDENTURE made this thirty first day of Janry and first day of Febry 1714 between GEORGE STAPLETON Son of THOMAS STAPLETON of Christ Church Parish in Middlesex County of one part and ALEXANDER GRAVES of above Parrish and County Bricklayer Witnesseth that for ye sum of forty pounds Sterl. and of the sum of five shillings paid by sd Alexander Graves the said George Stapleton hath granted to him by force of the Statute for transferring uses into possession and to his heires One hundred and sixty acres of land in the Parish of Christ Church in County of Middlesex and bounded Begining at a Corner Stump of WILLIAM BROOKES thence Northwest to a Hickory by Capt. ROBERT DANIELL thence to a corner White oak of HENRY NICHOLLS to a begining red oak in THOMAS KIDDs line thence to a red oak at ATTWOODs line thence along the severall courses of said Attwoods line to Brookes line and soe to the beginning To Hold to him the said Alexander Graves and to his heires forever
In presence of us JOHN PRICE,   George Stapleton
     JOS. HARDEE, RICHD. STEEVENS
At a Court held for Middx. County the first day of Febry 1714
George Stapleton came this day into Court & acknowledged his Lease and Release for land to Alexander Graves which is admitted to record

pp. 368- 369   KNOW ALL MEN by these presents that wee ELIZABETH WATTS and JOHN GIBBS of Middx. County are bound unto MATTHEW KEMP Gentl. first in Comission of the peace for said County in sume of one hundred pounds Sterl. this first day of Febry 1714.
The Condition of this obligation is such that if Elizabeth Watts Administratrix of all the goods and credits of JOHN WATTS deced doe make a perfect inventory of said deced Estate when required and make a true account of her actings and doings therein when required and if it shall hereafter appear that any last Will and Testament was made by the said deced if said Elizabeth Watts doth deliver up her Letter of Administr: in ye said Court that then this obligation to be void otherwise to remain
In presence of us JOHN THACKER,   Elizabeth ℰ Watts
     JNO. CURTIS   John ☉ Gibbs
At a Court held for Middx. County the first day of Febry 1714
The above bond was presented in Court by the Subscribers to it & by them ackd. wch is ad. to record.

p. 369   KNOW ALL MEN by these presents that I WILLIAM EVANS of the County of Middlesex impower EDWARD PIERCE of same County to goe upon my Dwelling Plantation in said County and to occupie all the land belonging to me for term of three years and forthwith to take into his Custody all things belonging to me which are in the house wherein JOHN HUGHS is resident upon my said land as also Eight hundred pounds of Tobacco and Cask in the hands of said John Hughs due to me for rent and all household goods and things whatsoever which I left in possession of him the said John Hughs at or upon my plantation as Witness my hand this 17th day of November 1714
Witness ARTHUR NASH,   William ⋁ Evans
     THOMAS T CURLIS
At a Court held for Middlesex County the first day of February 1714
This Power of Attorney from William Edwards to Edwd. Pierce was proved in Court by the oathes of Arthur Nash and Thomas Curlis and admitted to record

pp.   THIS INDENTURE made the thirty first day of January 1714 and the first day of
369-   February 1714 Between JAMES MEACHAM of County of Middlesex of one part and
371   JOHN VIVION Gentl. of same County Witnesseth that said James Meacham for sum
        five shillings paid by said John Vivion doth sell unto said John Vivion land in
Middlesex County containing One hundred and thirty acres bounded begining at a Poplar standing by a branch side near the head of the South Fork of Wadeing Muddy Creek
and runing from thence North to a marked white oak at the head of a valley and down
the valley unto the head of the North fork of said Wadeing Muddy Creek being in the
Parish of Christ Church in County aforesaid & now in occupation of said John Vivion to
hold for term of six months to the end that by vertue of the Statute for transferring
uses into possession the same can be released Now This Indenture Witnesseth that said
James Meacham for sume of forty five pounds lawfull money Sterl. and one thousand
pounds of Legall sweet scented Tobacco paid by said John Vivion said James Meacham
hath granted unto said John Vivion all the aforesd parcell of land
In presence of us JN. THACKER,   James Meacham
        THO: VIVION; WILLIAM LAWSON,
        JOHN SMITH, MARY _M_ GOODWIN (Lease)
    At a Court held for Middlesex County the first day of March 1714
James Meacham came into Court & acknoweldged the above lease and release to John
Vivion which is admitted to record MARY MEACHAM also the Wife of said James came
this day into Court & relinquished her right of Dower in said land which is hereby
Certifyed
KNOW ALL MEN by these presents that I James Meacham am bound unto John Vivion
in the sum of Ninety pounds Sterling money of Great Brittain and two thousand pounds
of good legall sweet scented Tobacco this first day of February 1714.
    The Condition of this obligation is such that if James Meacham truely keep all articles
contained in Indenture that then this obliglation to be void otherwise to remain
In presence of us JN. THACKER,   James Meacham
        THO: VIVION, WILLIAM LAWSON
    At a Court held for Middlesex County the first day of March 1714
James Meacham came into Court & acknowledged the above bond which is admitted to
record

p.   KNOW ALL MEN by these presents that wee WM. SANDIFORD, ROBERT DUDLEY &
371   JOHN MARSTON of County of Middlesex are bound unto CHRISTOPHER ROBINSON
        gent first in commission of the peace for said County in sum of three hundred
pounds Sterl. this 5th day of Aprill 1715.
    The Condition of this obligation is such that if Wm. Sandiford Executor of the last Will
and Testament of JOHN SANDIFORD deced do make Inventory & exhibit same in Court and
truely administer the Estate according to Law that then this obligaltion to be void
otherwise to remain
In presence of us   JOHN CURTIS,   William Sandiford
        WIL. STANARD   Robt. Dudley   Jno. Marston
    At a Court held for Middx. County the 5th of April 1715
The above Bond was acknowledged by the subscribers to it and admitted to record

pp.   KNOW ALL MEN by these presents that wee ELIZABETH ALLEN, JAMES MEACHAM
371-   and JOHN BATCHELDER of County of Middlesex are bound unto JOHN SMITH gent
372   first in commission of the peace for said County in sum of five hundred pounds
        this first day of June 1715.
    The Condition of this obligation is such that if Elizabeth Allen Executrix of the last Will

and Testament of RICHARD ALLEN deceased do make a true and perfect inventory and exhibit the same in ye County Court and truely administer the Estate according to Law that then this obligation to be void otherwise to remain in force

In presence of HARRY BEVERLEY,   Eliza. Allen
           THO:SMITH   James Meacham   John Batchelder

At a Court held for Middx. County the 7th day of June 1715
This bond was acknowledged in Court by the Subscribers to it and admitted to record

p. 372   KNOW ALL MEN by these presents that wee GEO: WORTHAM, JNO. VIVION & WIL. STANARD gent are bound unto our Sovereign Lord the King in the sum of one thousand pounds Sterl. this 7th day of June 1715.

The Condition of this obligation is such that if George Wortham is by Virtue of a Comission from Ye. Honble ALEXANDR: SPOTSWOOD his Majts. Lt. Governor & Comandr. in Cheife of this Dominion of Virginia appointed Sheriff of aforesaid County of Middx. for this ensueing year Now if George Wortham Sheriff shall at all times render unto the Auditor the full account of all his Majts. Revenues in said County of Middlesex and due payment make of all publick & county dues as shall be leveyed and return a list or rent role to his Majesties Auditor that then this obligation to be voyd else to stand

In presence of JNO. CURTIS   George Wortham
                                  Jno. Vivion   Wm. Stanard

At a Court held for Middx. County the 7th day of June 1715
The within bond was acknowledged by the subscribers to it and admitted to record

pp. 373-375   THIS INDENTURE made the 6th and 7th day of June 1715 Between HENRY NICHOLLS of County of Middlesex of one part and JOHN SEGAR of same County Witnesseth that Henry Nicholls for sum Twenty shillings lawfull money of England sold unto said John Segar One hundred and eleven acres of land in the Parish of Christ Church in County of Middlesex being part of a Patent for Five hundred and thirty acres of land granted to HENRY NICHOLLS SENR. deced and now in possession of Henry Nicholls Junr. and bounded begining at a Spanish Oak standing on side of a hill running thence South to a Corner red oak which divides the said land and land of JOHN PRICE thence runing South West to the begining place To Have and to hold unto the said John Segar for one year to the intent that by virtue of the Statute for transfer-ring uses into possession that said John Segar may be in actuall possession of said land Now This Indenture Witnesseth that said Henry Nicholls for sum of Twenty five pounds Sterling money of England hath sold unto John Segar and his heirs forever the afore-said one hundred and eleven acres of land

In presence of JNO. VIVION,   Henry Nicholls
         ROBT. PARROTT, RICHD. PERROTT

At a Court held for Middlesex County the 5th day of July 1715
Henry Nicholls came into Court and acknowledged the above lease and release which is admitted to record ALICE NICHOLLS also the Wife of said Henry Nicholls appeared in Court & relinquiahed her right of dower which is hereby certifyed

KNOW ALL MEN by these presents that I HENRY NICHOLLS am bound unto JOHN SEGAR in the sum of one hundred pounds Sterling money of England this 7th day June 1715.

The Condition of this obligation is such that if Henry Nicholls shall truely keep all agreemts. mentioned in Indentures that then this obligation to be void otheways to stand

In presence of JNO VIVION,   Henry Nicholls
       ROBT. PERROTT, RICHD. PERROTT

At a Court held for Middx. County the 5th day of July 1715
Henry Nicholls presented this bond in Court which was admitted to record

pp.   THIS INDENTURE made the second and third day of January 1715 between
375-   RICHARD STEEVENS and SARAH his Wife of Middlesex County and Parish of Christ
376   Church of one part and JOHN GRYMES of same Witnesseth that Richard Steevens
       and Sarah his Wife for sum of Sixty pounds lawfull money of Great Britain have
sold unto said John Grymes Five hundred acres of land in Middlesex County where he
the said Stevens now lives where is seized in fee simple by descent from MICHAEL MUS-
GROVE deceased to whom the same was granted by Patent dated the 28th day of Aprill
1691 all which said land are now in possession of said John Grymes by vertue of bar-
gain and sale for term of six months and of the Statute for transferring uses into
possession
In presence of CHARLES GRYMES,   Richd. Steevens
     WALKER WINGFIELD, JANE BURWELL   Sarah + Steevens
 At a Court held for Middlesex County the 3d day of January 1715
Walker Wingfield and Charles Grymes came into Court and made oath that they saw
Richard Steevens and Sarah Steevens sign and deliver the above lease and release to
John Grymes Gent which is admitted to record.
 At a Court held for Middlesex County the 7th day of February 1715
Richard Steevens came into Court and acknowledged his lease and release which is ad-
mitted to record. Sarah Steevens also the Wife of said Richard this day appeared and
voluntarily relinquished her right of dower which is hereby certified

p.   KNOW ALL MEN by these presents that we EDMUND HAMERTON, WILLIAM
377   STANARD and GARRITT MINOR of Middx. County are bound unto Capt. JOHN
     SMITH gent first in comission of the peace for said County in sum of Sixty
pounds Sterling money this Fifth day of July 1715.
 The Condition of this obligation is such that if Edmund Hamerton (Administrator of
RINGING GARDNER deceased) doe make a true Inventory of said deced Estate and truely
administer the same according to Law and further if it shall appear that any last Will
and Testament was made by the said Deced sd Edmund Hamerton being required do deliver up his letters of administration that then this obligation to be void otherwise to
remain
In presence of us JNO. VIVION,   Edmund Hamerton
     ZACH. LEWIS   Wil: Stanard   Garritt Minor
 Ackd. in Court the 5th day of July 1715 by the subscribers & admitted to record

p.   KNOW ALL MEN by these presents that wee WM. KILPIN & WILLIAM STANARD
377   are bound unto our Sovereign Lord King George in sum of ten thousand pounds
     of Tobacco this 2d day of August 1715
 The Condition of this obligiation is such that Whereas Wm. Kilpin hath obtained a Lycence to keep and ORDINARY at his house in URBANNA therefore if he doth constantly
provide good and cleanly lodging and dyett for travellers and stableage fodder and
provender or pastureage for their horses as the seasons require dureing the term of
one year from the 2d day of August 1715 and shall not suffer unlawfull gameing nor on
the Sabbath suffer any person to tipple more than is necessary that then this obligation to be void otherwise to remain
In presence of MATT PARRY,   W. Kilpin
     JOHN SEGAR   Wil. Stanard

At a Court held for Middx. County the 2d day of August 1715
This bond was presented in Court by the Subscribers to it and admitted to record

pp.   Virginia SS By His Maties Lt. Governour & Comander in Cheif of this Dominion
377-   a Proclamation for enforceing the Laws for the better Regulateing the manner
378   of signing & certifying Propositions and Grievances to the Generall Assembly.
WHEREAS the Act made at a Generall Assembly held at James City ye 8th day of
June 1680 entituled An Act for Presentation & delivery of Grievances and still unre-
pealed hath been so much neglected and issued that notwithstanding the plain
directions therein given for preventing ill disposed persons from transmitting to the
Generall Assembly Scandalous Seditious papers under ye Generall name of Grievances
of ye Countys wherein the Subscribers dwell although the same be unknown to ye
greater part of his Majts. good Subjects of the Countys whose title they bear I have received information that such has been the licentious practices of diverse evill disposed
persons of late that scandalous and seditious papers have been framed and ye names of
divers persons put thereto, and others have been handed about through the Countys
and ye meaner sort of people called together in a riotous manner to sign the same and
ye sd papers called by the generall name of the Grievances of the freeholders or Inha-
bitants of such County not signed at ye Court appointed for Certifying such grievances
as the said Act directs nor presented by the persons signing ye same but only by one or
two of ye sd Subscribers have been certifyed by the Justices of such Courts altho it
could not appear to them whether the names affixed thereto were really ye writeing of
the persons said to be subscribers, Neither doth it appear by ye Certificates annexed
thereto whether ye same be the generall Grievances of the Countys or only of the
persons subscribing nor which of the subscribers did present the same by which evill
practice the minds of his Matys good Subjects have been seduced by private insinu-
ations of crafty evill designeing men the good intention of ye sd Act evaded and the
time of ye Generall Assembly to ye Great burthen of Ye Country spent in reading trife-
ling propositions or such papers as require rather ye punishments of ye Authers than
to be considered as Grievances For prevention whereof for ye future And to ye and the
propositions & just Grievances of ye people may be presented in a decent manner and
regularly certified I have thought fit by & with the advice and consent of his Majts.
Councell to issue this Procalamation HEREBY strictly chargeing and requireing all Justices of ye Peace within this Colony that they diligently observe the directions of the
aforerecited Act and that they certifie no grievances but such as shall be signed at ye
time & place therein appointed and duely presented by ye persons signing the same
and ye sd Grievances being so signed and presented they shall cause to be attested as
the grievances of the persons signing and presenting ye same as by the aforementioned Act & Clauses in the Act for regulateing the Election of Burgesses & passed in ye
year 1705 is injoyned & directed. And Whereas the power of redressing ye Just grei-
vances of ye peoples is lodged in the Generall Assembly consisting of ye Governour
Councell and Burgesses and not in either of the houses of the Assembly seperately I doe
further with ye advice aforesaid direct & appoint that all such propositions and grievances as shall be legally signed and presented in the manner aforesaid to be certified
to the Generall Assembly as by Law they ought to be and to ye end all riotous tumultous
meetings for frameing & signing such propositions & grievances may be prevented I
doe hereby strictly charge & require all Magistrates within this Colony that they use
their utmost diligence to discover and punish all such persons their aiders & abettors as
shall be found to assemble in a riotous manner for drawing up or signing papers
under ye name of Grievances otherwise than the laws in that case directs and I doe appoint this Proclamation to be read and published by the Sheriffs at the Courthouse of

every County at the first Court held in ye sd County after ye receipt thereof and to be
entred upon ye records of there respective County Courts together with the Writts for
the Election of the Burgesses and at the Court of Claims.
  Given at the Councill Chamber in Williamsburgh the 24th August 1715 in the second
year of his Majts Reign.
          GOD SAVE THE KING   A.SPOTSWOOD
  At a Court held for Middx. County the 4th October 1715
This Proclamation was this day read in Court & admitted to record

pp.   THIS INDENTURE made the Sixth day of June and the 28th day of June 1715 Be-
379-   tween RICHARD STEEVENS of Christ Church Parish in County of Middlesex Plan-
381   ter of one part and JOHN SMITH of the same County Planter Wittnesseth that said
         Richard Steevens by Indenture this Sixth day of June for consideration ex-
pressed (Twenty Shillings) did sell unto said John Smith lands with a Plantation containing Three hundred acres in Parish of Christ Church and Middlesex County being
part of a Patent granted to Lieut. JOHN NEADLES for Five hundred and fifty acres and
now in occupation of Richard Steevens and bounded Begining at an ancient corner
pine trees in the fork of a creek opposet to STONE POINT Devedent thence up said Creek
to a red oak commonly known by name of Sr. HENRY CHICHELEYs Corner tree at head of
said creek thence by a line of marked trees lately surveyed to Barbeque Creek then
along a line to ARMSTEDs land and runing the Course of said late survey includeing
three hundred acres of land To Hold said land unto John Smith for term of one year to
the end that said John Smith might be in actuall possession Now This Indenture Witnesseth that said Richard Steevens for sum of fifty five pounds Sterling of England doth
sell unto said John Smith in his actuall possession all the Estate right of said land
In presence of GEO: HARDIN,   Richd. Steevens
       WM. SANDEFORD, CHR: SUTTON   J. Smith
  At a Court held for Middx. County the 6th day of December 1715
Richard Steevens came into Court & acknowledged the above lease and relelase to John
Smith which is admitted to record
  KNOW ALL MEN by these presents that I Richard Steevens am bound unto John Smith
in the sum of five hundred pounds Sterling money of England this 28th June 1715.
  The Condition of this obligation is such that if Richard Steevens truely keep all
articles to be kept in a certain Indenture that then this obligation to be voyd otherwise
to stand
In presents of GEO: HARDIN,   Richd. Steevens
       WM. SANDIFORD, CHR: SUTTON
  At a Court held for Middx. County the 6th day of Decembr: 1715
Richard Steevens acknowledged the above bond which is admitted to record

p.   MDME. the following appraismt. was made in pursuance of an Order of Middx.
382   County Court dated the Seventh day of June 1715 made in a Suit of Attachmt. be-
         tween WILLIAM STANARD Plt and THOMAS CRANK Defendt. hoges appraisd by
Vertue of attachment for use of Mr. Willm. Stanard belonging to the Estate of Thomas
Crank Junr. by me   MATT PERRY S:S:M:C:
         1 white sow, 1 read do; 3 young barrows, 1 black barrow could not be takeing
total 260.
  At a Court held for Middx. County the 7th day of December 1715
This Appraismt. was admitted to record

p.   KNOW ALL MEN by these presents that we GEORGE WORTHAM, JOHN ROBINSON are
382   bound to our Sovereign Lord the King in sum of Seventy six thousand seven
        hundred ninty eight pounds of Toba: this seventh day of December 1715.
   The Condition of this obligation is such that if Geo: Wortham Sheriff shall truely collect the publick & County Levys and pay unto respective County & Country creditors as
directed by Act of Assembly begun at her Majty Queen Anns Royall Capitoll the 23d day
of October 1705 then this Obligation to be voyd or else to stand
In presence of W. GOUGH   Geo: Wortham
                                                     Jno. Robinson
   At a Court held for Middx. County the 7th of December 1715
George Wortham & John Robinson acknowledged this their bond and it was admitted to
record.

pp.   KNOW ALL MEN by these presents that wee DAVID MORGAN, HUGH MACKTYRE &
382-   WM. GARDENER of Middlesex County are bound unto CHRISTOR: ROBINSON gent
383   first in Commission of peace for abovesaid County in sum of one hundred pounds
        Tobacco this 7th day of Febry 1715.
   The Condition of this obligation is such that if David Morgan (Administrator of THO-
MAS SMITH deceased) do make a true inventory of the said Estate and truely administer
the said Estate and it it should appear that any last Will and Testament was made by said
deced that said David Morgan doe deliver up his Letters of Admon. that then this obli-
gation to be voide otherwise to remain
In presence of WM. STANDARD,   David ⋀ Morgan
                                             Wm. W Gardner Hugh Macktyre
   At a Court held for Middx. County the 7th day of February 1715
The above bond was presented in Court & acknowledged & ordd. to be recorded.

pp.   THIS INDENTURE made this second and third ay of Aprill 1716 Between EDWARD
383-   LAWRANCE and ELIZABETH his Wife and ELIZABETH ROSE of ESSEX COUNTY of the
385   one part and HENRY BASKETT of County of Middx. of other part Witnesseth that
        sade Edward Lawrance and Elizabeth his Wife and Elizabeth Rose for sum of two
thousand and fifty pounds of good sweet sented Tobacco & Caske do sell unto said Henry
Baskett in his actuall possession by Virtue of bargaine and sale and by force of Statute
for transferring uses into possession a tract of land in Middx. County formerly conveyed by JOHN WILLIS to EDWARD DOCKER by Deed the 12th day of November 1683 and
by sade Edward Docker sold to NICHOLAS FOWLES as by an Assignment dated the 8th of
February 1685/6 as by Deed will appear in Middx. Court
In presence of us JNO. CURTIS,   Edward Ɛ Lawrance
        ABRAHAM ⊤ TRIGG, JNO. ⊢⊣ GUTRY   Elizabeth ⋎Ɫ Lawrance
   At a Court held for Middx. County the 3d day of Aprill 1716
Edward Lawrance and Elizabeth his Wife came into Court and acknowledged this lease &
release (the said Eliza. being first privately examined) which is admitted to record.
   KNOW ALL MEN by these presents that wee Edward Lawrance and Elizabeth his Wife of
ESSEX COUNTY are bound unto Henry Baskett in sum of fifty pounds Sterling money of
England this 3d day of Aprill 1716.
   The Condition of this obligation is such that if above bounden Edward Lawrance keep
harmless the above named Henry Baskett in certain parcell of land without hindrance
of said Edward Lawrance or Elizabeth his Wife that then this obligiation to be voyd or
else to stand
In presence of us JNO. CURTIS,   Edward Ɛ Lawrance
        ABRAHAM ⊤ TRIGG, JOHN ⊢⊣ GUTRY   Elizabeth ⋎⋎ Lawrance

At a Court held for Middx. County the 3d day of Aprill 1716
Edward Lawrance & Elizabeth his Wife acknowledged this bond which is admitted to
record.

p.   IN OBEDIENCE to an Order of the Middlesex County Corte beareing date the 7th of
385   March 1715 We being first sworn by Mr. CHRISTOPHER ROBINSON Gent one of his
        Mat. Just. of ye peace for sd County & in company with Mr. THOMAS COOKE Sur-
verr. have laid out ye land in difference between Capt. HENERY ARMESTED Plant. & Mr.
DUDLEY JOLLEY Defendt. according to the severall corses of a Patin belonging to Capt.
Henery Armested beareing date 1662 we find a Traspass committed within ye boundes of
sd Capt. Armested land one shilling Damage
Foreman   GEO; BARRICK   STOKLEY TOWLES   JOHN MAYO
   JOHN GIBBS   JON. MARSTON   JACOB STIFF
   JOS. GOARE   JNO. + MILLER   JOHN FEARN
   THOS. BRISTOW   PETER P BRUMELL   JOHN SMITH
   At a Court held for Middlesex County the 3d day of Aprill 1716
Admitted to record by Order of Court

p.   Mr. ZACHARY LEWIS and Mr. HARRY BEVERLEY Gent
385   I do hereby authorize you for me to appear as my Attorney in Middx. County
        Court in Aprill Court next and thereto confess Judgmt. to Mr. WILLIAM STANARD
for three hundred and sixty eight pounds of Tobacco wch I am indebted to him by Bill
and for your so doing this shall be yr sufficient warrant this 10th day of March 1715/6
Witness DIANA D UNDERWOOD   WILLIAM W-H HAMMETT

pp.   TO ALL TO WHOM these presents shall come I WILLIAM COCKE Esqr. his Majtys
385-   Secretary of State of Virginia send greeting. Know ye that I by virtue of his
386   Majestys Patents dated the Sixth day of May in the first year of his Majestys
        Reign have appointed WILLIAM STANARD Gentleman in the place & office of
Clerk of County of Middlesex Hereby requireing him to attend the Justices of sd County
at every Court to enter and draw up all orders and Judgments of Court & performe all
such acts as are insident to said place and office granting upon him full power to receive to his own proper use all fees, vailes, duties, priviledges & perquisites whatsoever
belonging to sd place or office hereby revoking all former Commission and reserving
to my self full power to make void this Commission. Given under my hand this 20th day
of April 1716 in second year of his Majesties Reign
A Commission to William Stanard Gent   Wm. Cocke
to be Clerk of Middlesex County
   At a Court held for Middlesex County the Fifth day of June 1716
This Commission to William Stanard to be Clerk of Middlesex County Court ordered to be
recorded
                              Test Wil Stanard ClCur
                                 Truely recorded Test R. HICKMAN D. ClCur

p.   KNOW ALL MEN by these presents that wee GEORGE WORTHAM & JOHN GRYMES &
386   EDWARD CLARKE of County of Middlesex are bound unto our Sovereign Lord
        George in sum of one thousand pounds Sterling this 5th day of June 1716.
   The Condition of this obligation is such that Whereas George Wortham is by Commission under the under of the Honble. Lt. Governour ALEXANDER SPOTSWOOD dated the 3d
day of May 1716 appointed Sheriff of County of Middlesex Now if George Wortham do
render unto Mr. Auditor LUDWELL all his Majts. Revenues dureing the time of his

Sherivalty and also due payment make of all dues as shall be leveyed unto the severall persons and faithfully perform the office of Sheriff that then this obligation to be voyd otherwise to stand

In presence of R. HICKMAN,   George Wortham
    WM. STANARD   John Grymes   Edwd. E͡ Clarke

At a Court held for Middlesex County the 5th day of June 1716
George Wortham, John Grymes & Edward Clarke acknowledged this bond to be their act and deed and it was admitted to record

pp. TO ALL TO WHOM these presents shall come I WILLIAM COCKE Esqr. his Majesties
386- Secretary of State of Virginia send greeting. Whereas WILLIAM STANARD Gent
387   Clerk of Middlesex County hath acquainted me that he hath business that re-
      quires his attendance in great Britain and hath made application to me to
appoint RICHARD HICKMAN Deputy Clerk under him in the said office dureing his absence Know Ye that I therefore do appoint said Richard Hickman Deputy Clerk of sd
Court giving to sd Deputy full power to perform the said office in the absence of sd Wm.
Stanard. Given this 27th day of April 1716.
  A Commission to Richd. Hickman to be   Wm. Cocke
  Deputy Clerk of Middlesex County

At a Court held for Middlesex County the fifth day of June 1716
This Comission to Richard Hickman to be Deputy Clerk of this County Court was ordered to be recorded

p.   KNOW ALL MEN by these presents that wee JOS. HARDEE, WILLIAM SEGAR and
387   WILLIAM SANDIFORD are bound unto our Sovereign King George in sum of ten
      thousand pounds of Tobo this 5th day of June 1716.

The Condition of this obligation is such that Whereas Jos. Hardee hath obtained a Licence to keep an ORDINARY at his house on the MAINE ROAD in County of Middlesex thereof if said Jos. Hardee doth provide good and cleanly lodgeing and dyett for travellers and stableage fodder and provender or pastureage for their horses as the seasons require during the term of one year from the 5th of June and not permitt any unlawfull gameing nor on the Sabbath to suffer any to drink more then is necessary that then this obligation to be void otherwise to remin

In presence of JAMES HIPKINGS,   Jos. Hardee
    JOHN BATCHELDER, WILLIAM DAVIS   Wil. Segar   William Sandiford

At a Court held for Middlesex County the 5th day of June 1716
Joseph Hardee, William Segar and William Sandeford acknowledged their bond and it was admitted to record

pp. THIS INDENTURE made the fourth and fifth day of June 1716 Between JONATHAN
387- JOHNSON of County of Middx. of one part and GABRIELL RAY of the same Witnes-
389   seth that Jonathan Johnson for sum Twenty pounds two shillings and nine
      pence Sterling hath sold unto Gabriell Ray in his actuall possession now by Vir-
tue of a bargain & sale and by force of Statute for transferring uses into possession One hundred acres of land in the Parish of Christ Church and County of Middx. and bounded Begining at a spanish oake standing in Iron Rock Levell at the head of a branch running from thence to a red oake that stands by the MAIN ROADE runing down ye Road to a Greate Chesnutt Corner tree of GEORGE BLAKEs land and adjoyning upon the land of ELIZABETH SMITH

In presence of JOHN OWEN 1716   Jonathan Johnson
    JOHN BRISTOW, JOSEPH ⊢⊣ ORPHAN

At a Court held for Middlesex County the fifth day of June 1716
Jonathan Johnson acknoweldged his lease and release to Gabriell Ray and it was admitted to record
    KNOW ALL MEN by these presents that I Jonathan Johnson am bound unto Gabriell Ray
in sum of Forty pounds Five shillings & Six pence this 5th day of June 1716.
    The Condition of this obligation is such that if Jonathan Johnson truely keep all
agreements in Indenture that then this obligation to be void otherwise to remain
In presence of JOHN OWEN 1716   Jonathan Johnson
        JOHN BRISTOW, JOSEPH ⊢⊣ ORPHAN
    At a Court held for Middx. County the fifth day of June 1716
Jonathan Johnson acknowledged his bond and it was admitted to record

p.   We the Subscribers have pursuant to an Order of Middx. County Court stated and
389   settled all accts. between EDWARD NUGENT and DAVID WILLIAMS and do find
        five hundred pounds of Tobacco due to Edward Nugent this 2d day of June 1716.
                            JNO. ROBINSON   HARRY BEVERLEY
Truely recorded R. HICKMAN D ClCur

pp.   THIS INDENTURE made the thirteenth and fourteenth day of July in ye year of
390-   our Lord God according to the accompt used in England 1716 Between JOHN
391   JOHNSON of County of Middlesex Planter of one parte and JOHN MARSTON of same
        County & Occupation of other parte Whereas said John Johnson by Indenture
dated the thirteenth day of this instant month of July for consideration expressed (five
shillings) did sell unto said John Marston all lands whereon said John Johnson now
liveth and formerly purchased of RICHARD STEEVENS containing One hundred acres in
County aforesaid and bounded begining att the narrows of STONE POINT & so runing up-
wards to the first branch beyond the said John Johnsons house on the North side of an
old field called SHEPHERDS GROUND & along to the head of said branch from thence
streight across to Richard Steevens line tree binding on ADAM CURTIS from thence to
the head of the forked branch & from thence along the South side of Stone Point to the
beginning To Hold for one year to the intent by virtue of the Statute for transferring
uses into possession said John Marston may be in actuall possession of said land NOW
THIS INDENTURE WITNESSETH that for sum of Twenty five pounds lawfull money of
England paid John Johnson hath granted said one hundred acres of land unto John
Marston forever to the use of the said John Marston
In presence of JOHN DEGGE,   Jno: Johnson
        RICHD. STEEVENS, W. BLACKBOURNE
    At a Court held for Middlesex County the Seventh day of August 1716
John Johnson acknoweldged his lease and release unto John Marston which was ad-
mitted to record and ANNE the Wife of said John Johnson appeared in Court & relin-
quished her right of Dower in the land which was also admitted to record
    KNOW ALL MEN by these presents that I John Johnson am bound unto John Marston in
the penal sum of one hundred pounds this Fourteenth day of July 1716.
    The Condition of this obligation is such that if John Johnson truely keep all articles
mentioned in Indenture that then this obligation to be void otherwise to remain
In presents of us JOHN DEGGE,   John Johnson
        RICHD. STEEVENS, W. BLACKBOURNE
    At a Court held for Middlesex County the 7th day of August 1716
John Johnson acknowledged this bond and it was admitted to record

pp.   THIS INDENTURE made the thirteenth and fourteenth day of March in the year
392-   of our Lord according to the Accompt used in England 1715 between JOHN MAR-
393   STON of County of Middlesex Planter of one part and WILLIAM BLACKBURN of
        same Gentmt. Whereas John Marston by Indenture bearing date the thirteenth
day of March for consideration therein (five shillings) did sell unto William Blackburne all lands called Marstons Plantation it being all the land purchased of JAMES
DUDLEY by THOMAS MARSTON deceased Father to the said John Marston containing One
hundred and fifty acres of land near the lower Chapell & marked & bounded Beginning
att a marked read oake a Corner tree on the MAIN ROAD which devides said land & the
lands of FRANCIS DODSON and so runing by a line of marked trees from thence to the
line of WILLIAM HACKNEY along Hackneys line of marked trees to the land of GEORGE
BARRICK & from thence along Barricks line to the main road & so down the road to its
first beginning place To Hold the said land for term of one year to the intent that by
virtue of the statute for transferring uses into possession the said William Blackburne
may be in actuall possession of said land NOW THIS INDENTURE WITNESSETH that in consideration of the sum Forty Seaven pounds Ten shillings lawfull money of England the
said John Marsten doth grant unto said William Blackburne his heires forever the said
one hundred and fifty acres of land
In presents of us JNO. JOHNSON,   John Marston
     RICHD. STEEVENS, WILLIAM /X\ FURNETT
At a Court held for Middlesex County the 7th day of August 1716
John Marston acknowledged his lease and release unto William Blackburne and it was
admitted to record and MARY the Wife of the sd John also appeared in Court and relinquished her right of Dower in said land which was admitted to record

p.   WHEREAS by an Order of Middlesex County Court dated the 3d day of Aprill 1716
393   CHR: ROBINSON, JOHN ROBINSON & JAMES WALKER or any two were desired to
        settle account in difference between WM. GORDON Plt. and EDMUND RYAN Deft.
between that & next Court but not haveing an opportunity of doing it at ye time mentioned in the said order; We the Subscribers have this day (at the request & with the
consent of the partys abovementioned) met & haveing audited & settled all accounts doe
find a ballance due to the Plaintiff of Seaven pounds Seaven Shillings & Four pence
wch sums the Deft. stands indebted & ought to pay to ye Plt: this 21st day of May 1716.
                        JNO. ROBINSON   JA: WALKER

pp.   KNOW ALL MEN by these presents that I WILLIAM STANARD of the County of
393-   Middlesex in Virginia Gent. intending shortly to proceed on a Voyage to great
394   Britaine have appointed CHICHELEY CORBIN THACKER, BARTHOLOMEW YATES and
        ROBERT BEVERLEY of Colony aforesaid gentlemen my Attorneys to demand and
receive from every person all sums of mony tobacco goods which shall be due to me and
upon refusal in my name to prosecute granting my said Attorneys full power to perform all I might do if personally present. In Witness I have set my hand & Seale the
Sixteenth day of May 1716
In presence of JNO. VIVION, JNO. CURTIS,   Wil. Stanard
     WIL. SEGAR, R. HICKMAN
At a Court held for Middlesex County the 7th day of August 1716
This letter of Attorney was proved in open Court by oathes of John Vivion, John Curtis,
William Segar & Richard Hickman the witnesses to it and admitted to record

pp.   THIS INDENTURE made this second day of October 1716 Between WM. SANDIFORD
394-   and FRANCES SANDIFORD his Wife of Parish of Christ Church & County of Middle-
395   sex of one part and JOHN BRADLEY of same Witnesseth that for sum Ten thou-
       sand pounds of sweet scented tobacco do sell unto said John Bradley in his
actuall possession by virtue off Indenture for one year and by force of the Statute for
transferring uses into possession all that plantation and land containing One hundred
acres in the Parish of Christ Church County of Middlesex and bounded begining at a
Gum tree on HOLLOWING POINT barr and thence up the Cove to a pine tree on the mouth
of the first branch thence to a corner pine joyning to ALLIMANs line thence to Sr.
HENRY CHICHELEYs Corner tree so bounding upon RICHARD STEEVENS, MADM. CHURCH-
HILL & HENRY ARMISTEAD To Hold the said premises unto John Bradley forever
In presence of us RICHD. STEEVENS,   William Sandiford
       THOMAS ᛒ DAVIS, JNO. JOHNSON 1716   Frances X Sandiford
At a Court held for Middlesex County the Second day of October 1716
William Sandiford and Frances his Wife acknowledged their lease and release (the said
Frances being first privately examined) and it was admitted to record.

pp.   THIS INDENTURE made the second and third day of July in the second year of the
395-   Reign of our Sovereign Lord King George now King of Great Britain 1716 Be-
398   tween MACKRORY SCARBROUGH of the County of Middlesex Planter of one part
       and HENRY ARMISTEAD of Parish of Kingston in County of GLOUCESTER Gentle-
man Witnesseth that for sum of fifty pounds of lawfull mony of Great Britain said
Mackrory Scarbrough hath sold unto said Henry Armistead in his actuall possession
now being by virtue of Indenture for one year and of the Statute for transferring uses
into possession and to the heires all those Two hundred acres of land in the County of
Middlesex in the Neck part of Three hundred acres of land by Survey formerly granted
by Patent of Sr. WILLIAM BERKELEY now in the tenure of ROWLAND MACKRORY and
was left by said Rowland Mackrory unto his Widow afterward married with one WIL-
LIAM NEEDLES who together with his Wife sold their right unto WILLIAM SCAR-
BROUGH from whom the said Mackrory Scarbroughs title derives which said Three
hundred acres are bounded beginning upon the South side of Rappahannock River
upon the land of GEORGE WADEING and runing West by North to the first specified place
which said Two hundred acres of land are to be compleatly laid of altogether next adjoining to other lands of said Henry Armistead in the County of Middlesex
In presence of BAR: YATES,   Mackrory ᴍ Scarbrough
       JOH: ROBINSON, JOHN GRYMES
At a Court held for Middlesex County the Fourth day of September 1716
Mackrory Scarbrough acknowledged this lease and release unto Henry Armistead Gentl.
and it was admitted to record

p.   KNOW ALL MEN by these presents that wee WM. GORDON and JOHN ROBINSON
398   Gentl. of Middlesex County are bound unto CHRISTOPHER ROBINSON, JAMES WAL-
       KER, JOHN GRYMES, OLIVER SEGAR, JOHN PRICE & JOHN VIVION Gentl. Justices of
the peace for said County in sum of one hundred pounds this 2d day of October 1716.
   The Condition of this obligation is such that if Wm. Gordon Administrator of BENJAMIN
KELLY deded do make a true inventory and further made a true account of his actings
and doing therein when thereto required and if it should hereafter appear that any last
Will and Testament was made by the sd deced ye sd Wm. Gordon being required to deliver up his Letters of Administration that then this obligation to be void otherwise to
remain

In presence of us W. GOUGH,   Wm. Gordon
              JNO. CURTIS   Joh: Robinson
     At a Court held for Middlesex County the 2d day of October 1716
Wm. Gordon & John Robinson gentl. acknowledged their bond and it was admitted to
record

pp.   KNOW ALL MEN by these presents that wee THOMAS MOUNTAGUE & GARRITT
398-   MINOR of Middlesex County are bound unto CH: ROBINSON, JOHN ROBINSON,
399   JAMES WALKER, JOHN GRYMES, OLIVER SEGAR, JOHN PRICE & JOHN VIVION Gentl.
         Justices of the peace for said County in sum of two hundred pounds Sterl. this
6th day of November 1716.
     The Condition of this obligation is such that ye above bound Thomas Mountague Ad-
ministrator of THOMAS STEELE deced do make a true inventory of said Estate and do make
a true account of his actings and doings therein when required by said Court and provided if it appear that any last Will and Testament was made by sd deced sd Thomas
Mountague being required do deliver up his Letters of Administration that then this
obligation to be void otherwise to remain
In presence of us .GEO: WORTHAM,   Thomas Mountague
              JNO. CURTIS   Garritt Minor
     At a Court held for Middlesex County the 6th day of November 1716
Thomas Mountague and Garritt Minor acknowledged their bond and it was admitted to
record

p.   KNOW ALL MEN by these presents that wee GRACE NICHOLSON, GEORGE WORTHAM
399   & MATTHEW HUNT of Middlesex County are bound unto CHR. ROBINSON, JOHN
         ROBINSON, JAMES WALKER, JOHN GRYMES, OLIVER SEGAR, JOHN PRICE & JOHN
VIVION Gentl. Justices of said County in sum of Three hundred pounds Sterl. this 6th day
of November 1716.
     The Condition of this obligation is such that if Grace Nicholson Administratrix of all
the goods, chattels and credits of JOHN MICKLEBURROUGH deced do make a true and perfect inventory of all estate and truely administer according to law and make a true account of her actings and doings therein and if it should appear that any last Will and
Testament was made by ye sd deced if Grace Nicholson do deliver up her Letter of Administration that then this obligation to be void otherwise to remain in full force
In presence of JNO. CURTIS,   Grace G Nicholson
                                        Geo: Wortham   Mat: Hunt
     At a Court held for Middlesex County the 6th day of November 1716
Grace Nicholson, George Wortham & Matthew Hunt acknowledged their bond and it was
admitted to record

pp.   THIS INDENTURE made this fifth and sixth day of Novembr: 1716 Between THO-
399-   MAS KIDD of the Parish of Christ Church and County of Middlesex of one part
401   and THOMAS HACKETT of same Witnesseth that for a valuable sum to him paid or
         secured to be paid doth grant unto said Thomas Hackett in his actuall possession
by virtue of bargain and sale for one year and by force of Statute for transferring uses
into possesion Sixty acres of land in County of Middlesex bounded begining at a Gum
tree by the MAIN ROAD side in the White Marsh being a line tree betwixt the said Thomas Kidd and JOHN ALLDIN and runing along sd line of Thomas Kidd and John Alldin
from the road to the NEGRO ROAD to the line of land formerly sold by said Thomas Kidd
to ROBERT NORMAN and now belonging to the Estate of Mr. HENRY THACKER deced and
runing along the line of the said land towards the Dragon Swamp thence along the line

of said Thomas Kidd till it come to a branch by side of an old field in which old field
there formerly stood a Tobacco house belonging to ROBERT BLACKLEY and so baring the
bredth toward the Main Road which will include Sixty acres of land To Hold unto said
Thomas Hackett and his heires

Testus JOHN ALLDIN,   Tho: Kidd
        FRANCES (her X mark) ALLDIN
        MARTHA /M TUGLE

At a Court held for Middlesex County the Sixth day of November 1716
Thomas Kidd acknowledged his lease and release unto Thomas Hackett and it was
admitted to record and ALICE the Wife of said Thomas Kidd appeared in Court and relinquished her right of Dower in said land which was also admitted to record

KNOW ALL MEN by these presents that I Thomas Kidd am bound to Thomas Hackett in
sum of Seven thousand five hundred pounds of Legall good sound sweet scented Tobacco and Caske this Sixth day of November 1716.

The Condition of this obligation is such that if said Thomas Hackett shall from hereafter enjoy the said Sixty acres of land without challenge that then the above bond to
be void otherwise to stand

In presents of us JOHN ALLDIN,   Tho: Kidd
        FRANCES X ALLDIN, MARTHA /M\ TUGEL

At a Court held for Middlesex County the 6th day of November 1716
Thomas Kidd acknowledged his bond which was admitted to record

p.   KNOW ALL MEN by these presents that we ALICE MASSEY & THOMAS CHOWNING
401   of Middlesex County are bound unto the Justices of the said County in sum of one
        hundred pounds Sterl. this 4th day of December 1716.

The Condition of this obligation is such that if ye above bound Alice Masy Administratrix of RALPH MASY deced do make a perfect Inventory & a true account of her actings
and doings therein when required and if it shall appear yt: any last Will and Testament
was made by ye sd deced if sd Alice Masy do deliver up her Letters of Administration
that then this obligation to be voyd otherwise to remain

                                            Alice A Masy
                                            Tho: T Chowning

At a Court held for Middlesex County the 4th day of December 1716
Alice Masy and Thomas Chowning acknowledged their bond & it was admitted to record

pp.   KNOW ALL MEN by these presents that we WM. GARDNER, JAMES MEACHAM &
401-   EDMOND MICKLEBURROUGH are bound unto CHRISTOPHER ROBINSON Gent first in
402   Comission of ye peace for County of Middlesex in sum of Sixty pounds Sterl. this
        4th day of December 1716.

The Condition of this obligation is such that if William Gardner do truely pay unto
ELIZABETH ALFORD Orphan of RICHARD ALFORD deced all Estate as shall be due said
Orphan as soon as she shall attaine to lawfull age and keep the Justices from trouble
about ye Estate that then this obligation to be voyd otherwise to remain

                        Wm. W Gardner
                James Meacham   E. Mickleburrough

At a Court held for Middlesex County the 4th day of December 1716
William Gordon, James Meacham and Edmund Mickleburrough acknowledged their
bond and it was admitted to record

p.   KNOW ALL MEN by these presents that wee NICHOLAS BRISTOW, JAMES BRISTOW,
402   THO: KIDD, WILLIAM BRISTOW, JOHN RHODES, THOMAS BRISTOW of County of
       Middlesex are bound unto the Justices of the said County in sum of five hundred
pounds Sterling this 4th day of December 1716.
   The Condition of this obligation is such that if Nicholas Bristow and James Bristow Executors of the last Will and Testament of JOHN BRISTOW deced make a perfect inventory
of all the Estate and a true account of their actings and doings therein and deliver all
the Legacys specified in sd Testament that then this obligation to be voyd otherwise to
remain

                         Nicholas Bristow   James Bristow
                         Tho: Kidd   Wm. Bristow
                         John Rodes   Thomas Bristow
   At a Court held for Middlesex County the 4th day of December 1716
This Bond was acknowledged and admitted to record

pp.   KNOW ALL MEN by these presents that wee THOMAS KIDD, ABRAHAM TRIGG and
402-   NICHOLAS BRISTOW of County of Middlesex are bound unto the Justices of the
403   said County in sum of Fifty pounds Sterling this 4th day of December 1716.
   The Condition of this obligation is such that if Thomas Kidd Executor of the last
Will and Testament of DANIELL TRIGG deced do make a true and perfect inventory of all
the Estate and a true account of his actings and doings therein and deliver all the Legacys Specified in the sd Testament that then this obligation to be voyd otherwise to
remain

                              Tho: Kidd
                         Abra: T Trigg Nicholas Bristow
   At a Court held for Middlesex County the 4th day of December 1716
This Bond was acknowledged and admitted to record

p.   KNOW ALL MEN by these presents that wee ELIZA. MINOR, OLIVER SEGAR and
403   THOMAS MOUNTAGUE of Middx. County are bound unto the Justices of the said
       County in sum of two hundred pounds Sterl. this first day of January 1716.
   The Condition of this obligation is such that if Elizabeth Minor Administratrix of
MINOR MINOR deced do make a true inventory of said Estate and do truely administer
according to Law and make a true account of her actings and doings therein and if it
shall appear that any Last Will and Testament was made by sd deced if sd Elizabeth
Minor being required do deliver up her letters of Administration that then this obligation to be void otherwise to remain

                         Eliza. E Minor
                         Oliver Segar   Thomas Mountague
   At a Court held for Middx. County the 1st day of January 1716
This bond was acknowledged and admitted to record

pp.   KNOW ALL MEN by these presents tht wee ELIZABETH DAVIS, STOKLY TOWLES,
403-   JOHN BATCHELDOR and ROBERT MURRY of County of Middx. are bound unto the
404   Justices of said County in sum of two hundred pounds Sterl. this first day of
       January 1716.
   The Condition of this obligation is such that if Elizabeth Davis Admr. with the Nuncu-
pative Will annext of JOHN DAVIS deced do make a true inventory of all the Estate and do
truely administer according to Law and deliver all the Legacys contained that then this
obligation to be voyd otherwise to remain

In presence of JNO. CURTIS,   Elizabeth Davis   John Batchelder
    W. GOUGH   Stokly Towles   Robert Murray
   At a Court held for Middlesex County the 1st day of January 1716
This bond was acknowledged and admitted to record

p.   KNOW ALL MEN by these presents that wee ANNE MAYO, STOKLY TOWLES & JOHN
404   LEWIS of Middlesex County are bound unto the Justices of the said County in the
      sum of two hundred pounds Sterl. this 5th day of Febry. 1716.
   The Condition of this obligation is such that if Anne Mayo Administratrix of VALEN-
TINE MAYO deced do make a true Inventory of all the said Estate and make a true
account of all her actings & doings therein and if it appear that any Last Will and Testa-
ment was made by the sd deced deliver up her letters of Administration that then this
obligation to be void otherwise to remain
In presence of JNO. CURTIS,   Ann *W* Mayo
    R. HICKMAN   Stokly Towles   John Lewis
   At a Court held for Middlesex County the 5th day of February 1716
This Bond was acknowledged and admitted to record.

pp.   KNOW ALL MEN by these presents that we THOMAS BROMWELL, DIANA BROM-
404- WELL, WILLIAM HACKNEY & JOHN BRADLEY of Middx. County are bound unto
405   the Justices of said County in sum of Fifty pounds Sterl. this fifth day of Febry
      1716/7. The Condition of this obligaiton is such that if Thomas Bromwell and
Diana Bromwell Administrators of NATHAN UNDERWOOD deced do make a perfect inventory of all the Estate and shall truely administer the same according to Law and if it
shall hereafter appear that any last Will and Testament was made by the sd deced that
the said Tho: & Diana shall deliver up their letters of Administration that then this obligation to be void otherwise to remain
                 Tho: Brumwell   Dianna *D* Brumwell
                 Wm. *⌒* Hackney   John Bradley
   At a Court held for Middlesex County the 5th day of February 1716
This Bond was acknowledged and admitted to record

p.   KNOW ALL MEN by these presents that wee RICHARD DANIELL, MATTHEW HUNT &
405   JOHN WATTS are bound unto our Sovereign Lord George in the sum of Ten thou-
      sand pounds of Tobacco this Sixth day of March 1716.
   The Condition of this obligation is such that whereas Richard Daniell hath obtained a
Lycence to keep an ORDINARY at this COURTHOUSE if said Richard Daniell doth con-
stantly provide good lodgeing and dyet for travellers and stableage fodder and proven-
der or paturage as the season require for their horses from sd sixth day of March 1716
and not permitt any unlawfull gameing or any to tipple more then is necessary on the
Sabbath day that then this obligation to be voyd otherwise to remain
In presence of JNO. CURTIS,   Richard Daniell
    W. GOUGH   Matthew Hunt   John Watts
   At a Court held for Middlesex County the 6th day of March 1716
This bond was acknowledged and admitted to record

p.   KNOW ALL MEN by these presents that I EDMOND MICKLEBURROUGH of Middlesex
406   County am bound unto THOMAS MOUNTAGUE of same County Junior in sum of
      Two hundred & fifty pounds current money this 5th day of Janry 1716/7.
   The Condition of this obligation is such that Whereas Thomas Mountague for the finall
determination of all Law Suites allready commenced or which hereafter be brought by

Edmond Mickleburrough his heirs against the said Thomas Mountague and GRACE his Wife (lately called GRACE NICHOLLSON) their heirs by reason of all or any part of ye Negroes or personall Estate of Mr. JOHN MICKLEBURROUGH deced which now is or which shall come to the hands of the said Thomas Mountague hath quietly surrendered unto the abovenamed Edmond Mickleburrough the following Negores that is to say one Negro man named Tony and one Negro woman named Sarah and the sume of Fifteen pounds in a Store with all his right to the same part of Negroes and personall Estate of the deceadant John Mickleburrough which now is or shall be in possession of Thomas Mountague and which may legally appertaine to Edmond Mickleburrough Now if the above bounden Edmond Mickleburrough at all tymes hereafter be contented with the named Negroes and money in lieu & full satisfaction of all other part of ye Negroes & personall Estate of the said Deceadant John Mickleburrough and also OF TOBIAS MICKLE-BURROUGH the said Deceadants Father deceased wch: now is or hereafter shall be in possession of Thomas Mountague and which may legally appurtaine to Edmond Mickle-burrough and shall permit Thomas Mountague at all times to hold the Negroes & per-sonall Estate of John Mickleburrough which is in possession of said Thomas Mountague without trouble if Edmond Mickleburrough shall at request of Thomas Mountague ack-nowledge this bond in Middlesex County Court that then this obligation to be void other-wise to remain

In presence of JOHN OWEN 1716   Ed: Mickleburrough
        OLIVER SEGAR, RICE CURTIS
   Att a Court held for Middlesex County the 5th day of March 1716
Edmond Mickleburrough acknowledged this Bond unto Thomas Mountague Junr: & it was admitted to record.

pp.   KNOW ALL MEN by these presents that wee MATTHEW KEMP, JOHN SMITH &
406-   GEORGE WORTHAM gent of County of Middlesex are bound unto the Justices of
407   said County in sum of Fifteen hundred pounds Sterl. this 5th day of March 1716.
         The Condition of this obligation is such that if Matthew Kemp Admr. with the
Will annexed of MATTHEW KEMP deced do make a perfect inventory of all the Estate and do truely administer the same according to Law and deliver all the legacys contained in the said Testament that then this obligation to be voyd otherwise to remain
In presence of W. GOUGH   Matt. Kemp
                                                     John Smith   Geo: Wortham
   At a Court held for Middlesex County the 5th day of March 1716
This bond was acknowledged and admitted to record.

p.   KNOW ALL MEN by these presents that wee JAMES WALKER, JOHN VIVION and
407   JOHN ROBINSON of County of Middlesex are bound unto the Justices of said County
         in sum of Six hundred pounds Sterling this first day of January 1716.
   The Condition of this obligation is such that if James Walker and John Vivion Execu-tors of the last Will and Testament of EDMUND HAMERTON deced do make a perfect in-ventory of said Estate and make a just account of their actings and doings therein and deliver all legacys contained in said Testament that then this obligation to be voyd otherwise to remain
In presence of W. GOUGH   Ja: Walker
                                                     Jno. Vivion   Joh: Robinson
   At a Court held for Middlesex County the 1st day of January 1716
This Bond was acknowledged and admitted to record.

pp.   THIS INDENTURE made the first day of April 1717 Between THOMAS BRISTOW &
407-   KATRIANE his Wife of County of Middlesex of one part and WILLIAM BLACK-
408   BURNE of same Witnesseth that said Thomas Bristow for sum of twenty five
        pounds Sterl. hath granted to farm lett all that land in Middlesex County & on or
near HEZEKIAH ROADES Mill Dam being part of a parcell of land devided between JOHN
ROADES & him ye said Thomas & given them by JOHN NICHOLLS deceased containing One
hundred and twenty one acres of land To Hold unto the full term of Ninety Nine years
from thence next ensueing paying yearly unto King George ye quitt rents and said
lands To Hold provided that if said Thomas Bristow shall truely pay unto said William
Blackburne the sum of twenty & five pounds Sterling on the twentyeth day of December in the year 1719 that then this present Indenture shall be void otherwise to stand
In presence of GEO: BARRICK,   Tho: Bristow
        EDWD. COUCH, MARY M BERRY   Katrane X Bristow
At a Court held for Middlesex County the second day of Aprill 1717
Thomas Bristow acknowledged his deed and it was admitted to record

pp.   KNOW ALL MEN by these presents that we SARAH ATWOOD, THOMAS KIDD & WIL-
408-   LIAM BROOKS of Middlesex County are bound unto the Justices of said County in
409   sum of Eighty pounds Sterling this second day of April 1717.
        The Condition of this obligation is such that if Sarah Atwood Administratr: of
RICHARD ATTWOOD deced do make a true inventory and further make a true account of
her actings and doings therein and if it shall afterwards appear that any last Will and
Testament was made by ye sd Deced that Sarah Attwood deliver up her letters of Ad-
ministration that then this obligation to be void otherwise to remain
In presence of W. GOUGH   Sarah + Attwood
                                            Tho: Kidd   Wm: Brooks
At a Court held for Middlesex County the 2d day of Aprill 1717
This bond was acknowledged & was admitted to record

p.   KNOW ALL MEN by these presents that we SARAH BOWDEN & PETER BRUMWELL
409   of Middlesex County are bound unto the Justices of said County in sum of one
        hundred pounds Sterl. this second day of April 1717.
    The Condition of this obligation is such that if Sarah Bowden Administratrix of GEORGE
BOWDEN deced do make a true inventory of all the Estate and truely administer the same
according to Law and if hereafter it doth appear that a last Will and Testament was made
by the sd Deced and Sarah Bowden being required deliver up her letters of Administration that then this obligation to be void or remain in full force
In presence of us W. GOUGH,   Sarah Ƶ Bowden
        ZACH: LEWIS   Peter D Brumwell
    At a Court held for Middlesex County the 2d day of Aprill 1717
This bond was acknowledged & admitted to record.

p.   KNOW ALL MEN by these presents that wee THOMAS MOUNTAGUE JUNR., JAMES
410   HIPKINGS & MATTHEW KEMP of Middlesex County are bound unto the Justices of
        said County this 7th day of May 1717.
    The Condition of this obligation is such that if Thomas Mountague Junr. & GRACE his
Wife Administrators of JOHN MICKLEBURROUGH deced doe make a true and perfect inventory of all goods and make a true account of his actings and doings therein and provided if hereafter it appear that any last Will and Testament was made by sd deced the sd
Thomas Mountague render up his letters of Administration that then this obligation to

be voyd otherwise to remain
In presence of W. GOUGH,   Tho: Mountague Junr.
                                        Matthew Kemp   James Hipkings
    At a Court held for Middlesex County the 7th day of May 1717
This bond was acknowledged and was admitted to record

p.   KNOW ALL MEN by these presents that wee WILLIAM WOOD & LEWIS TOMKIES are
410   bound unto our Sovereign Lord George in the sum of ten thousand pounds of To-
        bacco ye fifth day of March 1716.
    The Condition of this obligation is such that William Wood hath obtained a Lycence to
keep and ORDINARY in URBANNA Now if said William Wood constantly keep good and
cleanly lodgeing and dyet for travellers and stableage fodder and provender or pasturage as the seasons for require for their horses dureing the term of one year from the
fifth day of March 1716 and not suffer any unlawfull gameing nor on Sabbath day any
person to drink more than is necessary that then this obligation to be voyd otherwise to
remain
In presence of W. GOUGH   William Wood
                                                  Lewis Tomkies
    At a Court held for Middlesex County the 7th day of May 1717
This bond was acknowledged and it is admitted to record

pp.   THIS INDENTURE made this third day and fourth day of June in the year 1717 be-
411-   tween JOHN RHODES of County of Middlesex and ANNE his Wife of one part and
413   JOHN WORMELEY of County aforesaid Gent Witnesseth that said John Rhodes and
        Anne his Wife for sum of fifty pounds Sterling do sell unto said John Wormeley
that their CORN MILL and all that land on which same is erected in County of Middlesex
commonly called HEZEKIAH RHODES MILL and which descended to said John Rhodes as
Sonn and heir of said Hezekiah Rhodes late of this County deced To Hold by virtue of
Statute made for transferring uses into possession
In presence of us WM. W HACKNEY,   John Rhodes
    ALLICE E HACKNEY, JONATH: HIDE   Ann A Rhodes
    At a Court held for Middlesex County the fourth day of June 1717
John Rhodes and Anne his Wife acknowledged this their lease and release unto John
Wormeley Gent. and it was admitted to record. And ELIZABETH RODES appeared in Court
and relinquished her right of Dower which was also admitted to record.
    KNOW ALL MEN by these presents that I John Rhodes of Parish of Christ Church and
County of Middlesex am bound unto John Wormeley in sum of one hundred pounds Ster-
ling this fourth day of June 1717.
    The Condition of this obligation is such that if John Rhodes and Anne his Wife truely
observe all conditions mentioned in Indenture that then this obligation to be void or
else to remain
In presence of WM. W HACKNEY,   John Rodes
    ALLICE F HACKNEY, JONATH: HIDE
    At a Court held for Middlesex County the 4th day of June 1717
This Bond was acknowledged & it was admitted to record

pp.   THIS INDENTURE made the third and fourth day of June 1717 Between JOHN
414-   RHODES of County of Middlesex and ANNE his Wife of one part and ARMISTEAD
416   CHURCHHILL of County aforesaid Witnesseth that said John Rhodes and Anne his
        Wife for sum of Two hundred pounds of lawfull mony of England have sold unto
said Armistead Churchhill his heires forever land in County of Middlesex containing

Four hundred and ten acres the same having been formerly granted to HEZEKIAH
RHODES late of said County deced (Father to said John) by Patent dated the twenty ninth
day of Aprill 1693 and which after the death of said Hezekiah desended to said John as
Son and heir of said Hezekiah bounded begining at a white oak corner of WILLIAM
HACKNEYs land and runing thence South East to land of SR. WILLIAM SKIPWITH to a
Hickory thence North East to the land of Capt. MATTHEW KEMP to a stake in clear'd
ground thence by Kemps land East by North to a branch of Bonners Creeke to a great
Poplar in Kemps line thence down said branch North East to KILBEs land to a red oak
thence by Killbees line North West to said Hackneys line to a stake and lastly along
Hackneys line South East to the begining all said land Armistead Churchhill is now in
full possession by a bargaine and sale for one year and of Statute for transferring uses
into possession

In presence of MATT KEMP,   John Rodes
    JONATH: HIDE, WILLM: W HACKNEY

At a Court held for Middlesex County the fourth day of June 1717
John Rodes and Anne his Wife acknowledged this lease and release and it was admitted
to record. And ELIZABETH RODES also appeared in Court & relinquished her right of
Dower in the land conveyed by this Deed which is also admitted to record.

KNOW ALL MEN by these presents that I John Rhodes am bound unto Armistead
Churchhill in sum of four hundred pounds of lawfull mony of England the fourth day
of June 1717.

The Condtion of this obligation is such that if John Rhodes and Anne his Wife shall
truely keep all agreements mentioned in Indenture that then this obligation to be void
or else to remain

In presence of MATT KEMP,   John Rhodes
    JONATH: HIDE, WM. W HACKNEY

At a Court held for Middlesex County the 4th day of June 1717
John Rodes acknowledged this bond which is admitted to record

p.   KNOW ALL MEN by these presents that we ANNE RISKE, MATTHEW HUNT & JOHN
417   MURRY of County of Middlesex are bound unto the Justices of said County in sum
        of four hundred pounds Sterl. the fourth day of June 1717.

The Condition of this obligation is such that if Anne Risk Administratrix of JAMES
RISK deced do make a perfect inventory & exhibit the same in Court and make a true
account of her actings and doings therein when required and if hereafter it appear
that any last Will and Testament was made by the said deced that sd Anne Risk deliver
up her Letters of Administration that then this obligation to be voyd otherwise to
remain
In presence of W. GOUGH   Anne A Risk
                                            Matthew Hunt   John Murray

At a Court held for Middlesex County the 4th day of June 1717
This bond was acknowledged and it was admitted to record

pp.   KNOW ALL MEN by these presents that we MARY BRISTOW, HENRY GOODLOE &
417-   JOHN SEGAR of County of Middlesex are bound unto the Justices of said County in
418   sum of one hundred thirty five pounds Ten shillings & three pence half penny
        Sterl. this 4th day of June 1717.

The Condition of this obligation is such that if Mary Bristow Executrix of the last Will
and Testament of WILLIAM CARTER deced do make a true & perfect inventory of all
goods & exhibit the same into Court when required and also truely pay all the Legacys
contained in sd Testament that then this obligation to be voyde otherwise to remain

In presence of W. GOUGH   Mary ✗ Bristow
                                          Henry Goodloe   John Segar
  At a Court held for Middlesex County the 4th day of June 1717
This bond was acknowledged and admitted to record

pp.   THIS INDENTURE made the first and second day of July 1717 Between WILLIAM
418-   HACKNEY of County of Middlesex of one part and ARMISTEAD CHURCHHILL of
421   County aforesaid Witnesseth that said William Hackney for sum Thirty pounds
         Sterl. doth sell unto said Armistead Churchhill his heirs forever One hundred
acres of land in County of Middx. formerly the land of WILLIAM HACKNEY late of said
County deced (Grandfther of the said William party to these presents) who by his last
Will and Testament dated the thirtieth of September 1700 did devise said land to his Son
WILLIAM HACKNEY who was father to the said William Hackney Party to these presents
as by same proved in Court 7th day of July 1701 Bounded according to bound expressed
in said Will all which land are now in possession of said Armistead Churchhill by
Indenture bearing date the day before the date hereof and by force of the statute for
transferring uses into possession
In presence of MATT KEMP,   William W Hackney
     W. BLACKBURNE, JONATH: HIDE
  At a Court held for Middlesex County the 2d day of July 1717
William Hackney acknowledged this lease and release which is admitted to record.
  KNOW ALL MEN by these presents that I William Hackney am bound unto Armistead
Churchhill in sum of Sixty pounds lawfull money of great Britain this second day of
July 1717. The Condition of this obligation is such that if William Hackney truely keep
all the conditions mentioned in Indenture that then this obligation to be void otherwise
to remain
In presence of MATT KEMP,   William W Hackney
     W. BLACKBURNE, JONATH: HIDE
  At a Court held for Middlesex County the second day of July 1717
William Hackney acknowledged his bond which is admitted to record

p.   ALEXANDER SPOTSWOOD his Majesties Lieutenant Governour and Commander in
421   Cheif of the Colony and Dominion of Virginia to JAMES WALKER Gent
     By Virtue of the powers given me I do hereby authorize you to be Sheriff of
County of Middlesex dureing pleasure and I direct that you be sworn, and before you be
so sworn that you enter into bond before his Majesties Justices with two or more sufficient Securitys in penal sum of one thousand pounds Sterl. to render unto the Receiver Genll. and Auditor Revenues and full Acct. of all his Majts. revenue and dues in
same County dureing the time of your Sherivalty and also due payment make of all publick dues unto several persons appointed to receive the same and faithfull performance
make of all things belonging to the office of Sheriff and I command all his Majesties
officers Civil and Military and all subjects inhabiting the said County to be aiding to
you the said James Walker as Sheriff. Given under my hand and Seal of the Colony at
Wmsburgh the fourth day of May 1717 in the third year of his Majestys Reign
                  Seal   A. SPOTSWOOD
  KNOW ALL MEN by these presents that we JAMES WALKER, BARTHOLOMEW YATES &
WM. STANARD Gent of County of Middlesex are bound unto our Sovereign Lord George
in sum of one thousand pounds Sterling this 2d day of July 1717.
  The Condition of this obligation is such that Whereas James Walker is by Comission ap-
pointed Sherif of abovesaid County if therefore said James Walker do truely render all
his Majts. Revenues and also due payment make of publick dues as shall be levied and

faithfully perform his office of Sheriff that the above obligation to be voyde otherwise
to stand
In presence of R. HICKMAN,   Ja. Walker
    ZACH: LEWIS   Bar: Yates   Wil: Stanard
  At a Court held for Middlesex County the 2d day of July 1717
This bond was acknowedged by the subscribers and admitted to record

p.   VIRGINIA TO ALL TO WHOM these presents shall come Know Yee that I PETER
422   BEVERLEY Gentleman being appointed to Execute the office of SURVEYOR
      GENERALL of this Colony have commissionated THOMAS COOKE to be Surveyor of
Middlesex County dureing pleasure. In Witness I have sett my hand and Seale this
fourth day of June in the second year of the Reign of Lord King George Anno Domini
1717

                                    Peter Beverley   1716

p.   KNOW ALL MEN by these presents that I ALCE HACKNEY of County of Middlesex &
422   Wife of WM. HACKNEY of sd County do appoint my well beloved Brother JNO:
      ROADES of County of ESSEX my attorney to acknowlege all my dower of one hun-
dred acres of land in Middlesex County sold by my husband Wm: Hackney unto ARMI-
STEAD CHURCHHILL this 2d day of July 1717.
In presence of WILLIAM ROADS,   Alce T Hackney
    EZEKIAH ROADS, JOANER (hir × mark) HACKNEY
  At a Court held for Middx. County the 6th day of August 1717
This Letr. of Attorney was proved by Witness & admitted to record and John Roades by
Virtue relinquished Alice Hackney her right of Dower which is hereby Certified

pp.   KNOW ALL MEN by these presents that wee HANNAH MACKTYRE, THOMAS KIDD
422- & WILLIAM BROOKES of Middlesex County are bound unto Justices of said County
423   in sum of one hundred pounds Sterl. this 3d day of September 1717.
      The Condition of this obligation is such that if Hannah Macktyre Administra-
trix of JAMES MACKTYRE deced do make a true inventory of all the Estate and exhibit
the same in the County Court and perform and truely administer the same according to
law and if it shall hereafter appear that any last Will and Testament was made by said
deced that sd Hannah Mactyre be required do deliver up her Letter of Administration
that then this obligation to be voyde or else to remain
In presence of JONATH: HIDE,   Hannah Macktyre
    R. HICKMAN   Tho: Kidd   Wm. Brookes
  At a Court held for Middlesex County the 3d day of Septr 1717
This bond was acknowledged and admitted to record

p.   KNOW ALL MEN by these presents that we ARTHUR NASH, JOHN WILLIAMS, WIL-
423   LIAM DAVIS and CHARLES COOPER of County of Middlesex are bound unto the
      Justices of said County in sum of Two hundred pounds Sterl. this 3d day of Sep-
tember 1717.
      The Condition of this obligation is such that Whereas Arthur Nash Executor of the last
Will and Testament of JOHN NASH deced do make a true inventory of said deced & exhibit
the same in Court and made a true account of his actings & doings therein and also deliver all the legacys contained that then this obligation to be voyd otherwise to remain
                              Arthur Nash
                  John J Williams, Charles + Cooper

At a Court held for Middlesex County the 3d day of Septr 1717
This bond was acknowedged in Court and admitted to record

p.   KNOW ALL MEN by these presents that wee MANN PAGE of County of GLOUCES-
423   TER Esqr. and JOHN WORMELEY of County of Middlesex Gent as the Acting Execu-
       tors of MADM. ELIZA. CHURCHILL deced have made our Trusty Friend JONATH:
HIDE of County of Middlesex our Attorney to our use as Executors to receive of all persons mony now due and to make any acts necessary to recover such debts ratifying all
our said Attorney shall do likewise give our sd Attorney power of paying any debts formerly contracted by Madm. Eliza. Churchill in her life time. In Witness the 22d day of
August 1717
In presence of RICHARD EDWARDS,   Mann Page
        THOS. HAYES   Jno. Wormeley
    At a Court held for Middx. County the 3d day of Septembr: 1717
This Letr. of Attorney was proved in Court & admitted to record

pp.   THIS INDENTURE made this first and second day of November 1717 Between
424-   RICHARD PERROTT of County of Middx. Planter of one part and OLIVER SEGAR
427   Gent. of same County Witnesseth that said Richd. Perrott for five shillings law-
       full money Sterling doth acquit said Oliver Segar his heirs land in Middx. County
containing Two hundred and fifty acres beginning at a marked Chinkapin tree standing in the head of a branch of Parrotts Great Creek the next lowest branch to Mr.
RICHARD PERROTTs now Spring Branch thence down to too white oakes standing on the
head of a branch called the Flax Pond Branch thence down said branch into Muddy
Creek ALLIE WEEKES little Creek down along the said Creek thence up along Rappahannock River side until it meets with the mouth of Perrots Great Creek thence up the said
Creek to ye mouth of the Cove to the first begining place all which said tract of land in
Parish of Christ Church in County aforesaid and now in possession of Mrs. PENELOPE
PERROTT being laid off for her thirds or right of Dower To Hold unto said Oliver Segar
for term of six months to the end that by virtue of Statute for transferring uses into
possession said Oliver Segar may be in actual possession Now This Indenture Witnesseth that said Richard Perrot for sum of Seventy five pounds Sterling money doth
release unto said Oliver Segar aforesaid parcel of land
In presence of JNO. VIVION,   Richd. Perrott
        JOS. HARDEE, CATHERINE CARTER
    At a Court held for Middx. County the Sixth day of November 1717
Richard Perrot came into Court and acknowleged his lease and release which is
admitted to record
    KNOW ALL MEN by these presents that I Richard Perrott am bound unto Oliver Seager
in sum of one hundred pounds Sterl. money of Great Brittain this second day of November 1717. The Condition of this obligation is such that if Richard Perrott at all times
truely keep the agreements made in Indentur of lease and release and acknowledged in
open Court that then the above obligation to be voyd or else to stand
In presence of JNO. VIVION,   Richd. Perrott
        JOS: HARDEE, CATHERINE CARTER
    At a Court held for Middx. County the Sixth day of November 1717
This bond was acknowledged & admitted to record

pp.   KNOW ALL MEN by these presents that wee WILLIAM STANARD and MATTHEW
427-   KEMP of Middlesex County are bound unto the Justices of said County in sum of
428   Fifty pounds Sterl. the 6th day of November 1717.

The Condition of this Obligation is such that if William Stanard Administrator of
HENRY BARNES deced do make a perfect Inventory & exhibit the same in County Court
when required and shall render an account as Justices shall order and if it shall here-
after appear that any last Will and Testament was made by said deced and William
Stanard be required to deliver up his Letrs. of Administration that then this obligation
to be voyd otherwise to remain
In presence of ZACH. LEWIS   Wm. Stanard
                                                       Matt. Kemp
   At a Court held for Middx. County the 6th day of 9ber 1717
This bond was acknowledged & admitted to record

pp.   KNOW ALL MEN by these presents that we JOHN ROADS, WILLIAM HACKNEY &
428-   GEORGE BARRICK of County of Middlesex are bound unto the Justices of said
429   County in sum of five hundred pounds Sterling this 3d day of December 1717.
     The condition of this obligation is such that John Roads Admr. of HEZEKIAH
ROADS deced do make a perfect inventory of sd Estate and exhibit the same in County
Court and do make a true account of his actings and doings therein when required and
if it should appear that any any last Will and Testament was made by sd deced do deliver
up his Letrs. of Administration that then this obligation to be void otherwise to remain
In presence of WM. STANARD ClCur   John Roads
                                           Wm. W Hackney George Barrick
   At a Court held for Middx. County the 3d day of December 1717
This bond was acknowledged and admitted to record

pp.   THIS INDENTURE made the sixth and seventh day of October 1717 and in the
429-   fourth year of the Reign of our Sovereign Lord George Between ROBERT DUDLEY
433   of County of Middx. Parish of Christ Church of one part and AUGUSTINE SMITH
     of County of GLOSTER in Parish of Petso Witnesseth that said Robert Dudley for
sum of one hundred and sixty pounds Sterl. doth sell unto said Augustin Smith in his
actuall possession by virtue of sale maid for one year and by force of Statute for transferring uses into possession one tract of land in Parish of Christchurch and County of
Middlesex about Four hundred acres of land it being all the remainder of a certaine
tract and patent of land taken up and granted unto THOMAS DUDLEY and WILLIAM
ELLIOTT the patent dated the 21st of Aprill 1690 begining at a white oake on Bobs
Branch standing in line of marked trees belonging unto Mr. HARRY BEVERLEY and
runing several courses along said Beverleys and Mr. CHRISTOPHER ROBINSONs land into
the Green Branch down the Green Branch unto the land of Capt. HENRY ARMISTEAD
and by severall courses along said Armisteads land unto the begining place containing
Seven hundred and twenty two acres of land and sould by sail by Thomas Dudley & Wil-
liam Elliott unto Major ROBERT DUDLEY Father to sd Robert Dudley, excepting what sales
have been already made out of the Patent by Major Robert Dudley the father and Robert
Dudley the son
In presence of FR: WYATT,   Robt. Dudley
   CONGT. WYATT, JOHN READE
   At a Court held for Middx. County the third day of December 1717
Robert Dudley acknowledged his lease and release which is admitted to record ELIZA-
BETH DUDLEY the Wife of said Robert came into Court and relinquished her right of
dower in said land which is hereby certifyed
   This Bill bindeth me Robert Dudley to pay unto Augustine Smith the just sum of three
hundred and twenty pounds Sterl. on demand the condition is that if Robert Dudley do
confirm all the agreements in Deed of Lease and Release that then this obligation to be

void otherwayes to stand Signed this seventh day of October 1717
In presence of FR: WYATT,   Robt. Dudley
     CONGT. WYATT, JOHN READE
     At a Court held for Middx. County the third day of December 1717
This bond acknowledged and admitted to record

p.   MIDDLESELX COUNTY SCT. The DEPOSITION of PETER BRUMWELL is as followeth
433   Vizt. Which Deposition saith that he knoweth RICHARD PERROTT to be the Son of
       RICHARD PERROTT deced in the county aforesaid and first this Deponant saith
that he was a liver in the sd Richard Perrott Senrs. house wn: the said Richard Perrott
was born and that he was the reputed Son of Richard Perrott Senr. deceased and lawfully begotten
                                           Peter Brumwell
    Aprill 1st 1718. Sworn to in open Court and admitted to record.
    Middlesex County Sct. THE DEPOSITION of ELIANOR BRUMWELL is as followeth Vizt.
Which deposition saith that she was at the birth of Richard Perrott and saith that she
knows him the said Richard Perrott to be the reputed son of Richd. Perrott Senr. Deceast
and Lawfully begotten
    April 1st 1718   Elinor C Brumwell
    Sworn to in open Court and admitted to record
    Middlesex County Sct THE DEPOSITION of HENRY TUGGLE is as followeth Vizt. Which
Deposition saith that he knows Richard Perrott to be the known and reputed son of
Richard Perrott Senr. deced in the County aforesd and that he was lawfully begotten
    April 1st 1718   Henry Tugel
    Sworn to in open Court and admitted to record.

p.   KNOW ALL MEN by these presents that we ANNE ANDERSON and JOHN GRYMES
434   Gent of Middlesex County are bound unto Justices of said County in sum of one
       hundred pounds Sterl. this 7th day of Janry. 1717.
    The Condition of this obligation is such that if Anne Anderson Administratrix of
HENRY ANDERSON deced do make a perfect inventory of said deced Estate and exhibit the
same in County Court and do well and truely administer said Estate and if shall hereafter appear that any last Will and Testament was made by said deced that that being
required said Anne Anderson deliver up her said letters of Administration that then
this obligation to be void otherwise to stand
In presence of R. HICKMAN   An Anderson
                                           John Grymes
    At a Court held for Middlesex County the 7th day of January 1717
This bond acknowledged in Court and admitted to record

pp.   KNOW ALL MEN by these presents that we EDMUND MICKLEBURROUGH, ABRA-
434-   HAM TRIGG and THOMAS HACKET are bound unto CHRISTOPHER ROBINSON Gent
435   first in Comission of the peace for Middlesex County in sum of Five hundred
       pounds Sterl. this 7th day of Janry. 1717.
    The Condition of this obligation is such that if Edmund Mickleburrough shall pay unto
ANNE ALLEN Orphan of RICHARD ALLEN deced all estate due as soon as she shall attaine
to lawfull age that then this obligation to be voyd otherwise to remain
In presence of R. HICKMAN,   Edmd. Mickleburrough
     W. STANARD   Abra: | Trigg   Thomas Hacket
    At a Court held for Middlesex County the 7th day of Janry. 1717
This bond was acknowledged & admitted to record

p.   KNOW ALL MEN by these presents that we RICHINS BRAME, JOHN SEGAR and
435   WILLIAM GARDNER are bound unto CHRISTOPHER ROBINSON Gent first in Com-
        mission of the peace for said County in sum of one hundred pounds Sterl. this
7th day of Febry. 1717.
   The condition of this obligation is such that if Richins Brame shall truely pay unto
THOMAS BRAME and JAMES BRAME Orphans of JOHN BRAME deced all estate due said
Orphans as soon as they attaine to lawfull age and keep harmless the said Justices from
Estate that then this obligation to be void otherwise to remain
In presence of W. GOUGH   Richins Brame
                                           John Segar   William W Gardner
   At a Court held for Middlesex County the 7th day of February 1717
This bond was acknowledged in Court and admitted to record

pp.   THIS INDENTURE made the third and fourth day of February 1717 Between WIL-
436-   LIAM CHOWNING of Christ Church Parish in County of Middx. of one part and
438   JOHN MOSELEY of County aforesaid Witnesseth that said William Chowning for a
        valuble Consideration (five shillings) doth confirm unto John Mosely in his
actuall possession by virtue of sale for one year and by force of Statute for transferring
uses into possesion all that land containing Seventy six acres in Parish & County aforesaid and bounded beginning at a marked red oak standing by side of MATTHEW CRANKs
cleared ground runing thence South westwardly to a marked Dogwood by side of
MARVIN MOSELEYs Peach Orchard from thence Northwest to a white oak standing in
Moseleys line from thence Eastwardly to the first begining red oak
In presence of JOHN OWEN 1717   William Chowning
        WILLIAM BATCHELDER, GEORGE CHOWNING
   At a Court held for Middlesex County the 4th day of April 1718
This lease and release of land acknowledged and admitted to record
   KNOW ALL MEN by these presents that I William Chowning am bound unto John
Moseley in sum of one hundred pounds Sterling this fourth day of February 1717.
   The Condition of this obligation is such that if William Chowning truely keep all
articles mentioned in Indenture that then this obligation to be void otherwise to stand
In presence of JOHN OWEN 1717   William Chowning
        WILLIAM BATCHELDER, GEORGE CHOWNING
   At a Court held for Middx. County the first day of April 1718
This Bond was acknowledged & admitted to record

p.   KNOW ALL MEN by these presents that we RICHARD DANIEL, ABRAHAM TRIGG &
438   JOHN WATTS are bound unto our Sovereign Lord George in the sum of ten thou-
        sand pounds of Tobacco this 2d day of Aprill 1718.
   The Condition of this obligation is such that Whereas Richard Daniel has obtained a
Lycence to keep and ORDINARY at ye COURT HOUSE in this County Now if said Richard
Daniel constantly provide wholesome lodgeing and dyett for travellers and stableage
fodder & provender or pasturage as the season requires for their horses during term of
one year from the first day of Aprill 1718 and not permitt any unlawfull gameing nor
on the Sabbath day any person to drink more then is necessary that then this
obligation to be void otherwise to remain
In presence of JOHN CURTIS   Rich. Daniel
        JOS. HARDEE   Abraham T Trigg   John Watts
   At a Court held for Middx. County the 3d day of Aprill 1718
This bond was acknowledged and admitted to record

pp.   KNOW ALL MEN by these presents that we WILLIAM DAVIS, JOHN MOSELY &
438-   GEORGE CHOWINING are bound unto the Justices of Middlesex County in the sum
439   of one hundred pounds sterling this 1st day of April 1718.
     The Condition of this obligation is such that if William Davis, John Moseley &
George Chowning do truely pay unto CATHARINE ALLEN Orphan of RICHARD ALLEN
deced all Estate as shall be due said Orphan as soon as she shall attain to lawfull age that
then this obligation to be void otherwise to remain

In presence of JAMES COLE,   William Davis
    MATT: KEMP   John Mosely   George Chowning
   At a Court held for Middx. County the 1st day of April 1718
This Bond was acknowledged & admitted to record

p.   KNOW ALL MEN by these presents that we WILLIAM WOOD & LEWIS TOMKIES are
439   bound unto our Sovereign Lord George in sum of ten thousand pounds of Tobac-
    co this first day of April 1718.
The Condition of this obligation is such that Whereas William Wood hath obtained a
Lycence to keep an ORDINARY at his house in URBANNA Now if said Wm. Wood doth
provide good lodging and dyett for travellers and stableage fodder provender and
pasturage as the seasons require for their horses for one year from first day of April
1718 and not suffer any unlawfull gameing nor on Sabbath day any to drink more then
is necessary that then this obligation to be void otherwise to stand
                       William Wood
                       Lewis Tomkies
   At a Court held for Middx. County the 2d day of April 1718
This bond was acknowledged & admitted to record

pp.   KNOW ALL MEN by these presents that we JOSEPH HARDEE & MATTHEW KEMP are
439-   bound unto our Sovereign Lord George in the sum of ten thousand pounds of
440   tobacco this 2d day of April 1718.
     The Condition of this obligation is such that Whereas Joseph Hardee hath ob-
tained a Lycence to keep an ORDINARY in the County if therefore he doth constantly
provide good lodgeing and dyett for travellers and stableage fodder provender or
pasturage as the seasons require for their horses during term of one year from second
day of April 1718 and not permitt any unlawfull gameing nor on the Sabbath day suffer any to drink more then is necessary that then this obligation to be void otherwise to
remain

In presence of us JONATH: HIDE,   Jos. Hardee
    JON. PINNELL   Matt Kemp
   At a Court held for Middx. County the 2d day of April 1718
This bond was acknowledged in Court and admitted to record

p.   PURSUANT to an Order of Middx. County Court dated the 1st day of Aprill 1718 wee
440   the Subscribers did meet at the house of RICHARD ALLIN deced on the 3d day of
    May being first sworn before Mr. JOHN PRICE one of the Justices for said County
& did appraise a Neagroe girle named Sarah at the price of Six pounds Fifteen shillings

Currt. mony   Ed. Mickleburrough
                    John Alldin   Jno. Lewis
   At a Court held for Middx. County the 3d day of June 1718
This Return of Appraisement is admitted to record

p.   PURSUANT to an Order of Middx. County Court the 1st day of Aprill 1718 We the
440   Subscribers did meet at the House of ARTHUR DANALLY the 3d day of May and
      did view the outlett of Arthur Danally which is left him round EDMD. MICKLE-
BURROUGHs fence which we find to be not altogether the nearest way but not to much
inconvientry and sufficient for horse and bag or any Cart. Given under our hand
WILLIAM DAVIS
JOHN ALLDIN,   JNO. LEWIS
At a Court held for Middlesex County the 3d day of June 1718
This report admitted to record

p.   KNOW ALL MEN by these presents that wee PHILLIP WARWICK, THOMAS CHEY-
440   NEY & JOHN OWEN are bound unto the Justices of Middlesex County in the sum of
      two hundred and fifty pounds this 3d day of June 1718.
The Condition of this obligation is such that if Phillip Warwick truely pay unto MARY
GUTTRICH Orphan of JOHN GUTRICH deced all such Estate as shall appear to be due as
soon as she shall attain to lawfull age that then this obligation to be void otherwise to
remain   Philip Warwick
Thos: Cheney   Jno. Owen   1718
At a Court held for Middx. County the 3d day of June 1718
This bond was acknowledged and admitted to record

p.   KNOW ALL MEN by these presents that we ALICE NICHOLS, JOHN HARDEE & JOHN
441   WILLIAMS of Middx. County are bound unto the Justices of said County in sum of
      two hundred pounds Sterl. this third day of June 1718.
The Condition of this obligation is such that if Alice Nicholls Admtrx. of HENRY
NICHOLLS deced do cause to be made a true inventory and the same exhibit in County
Court and further make an account of her actings and doings therein and if it should
hereafter appear that any last Will and Testament was made by the sd deced she deliver
up her letters of Administration that then this obligation to be void otherwise to remain
In presence of MATT. KEMP,   Alice Nicholls
   THO: FIELD   John Hardee   Jno. Williams
At a Court held for Middx. County the 3d day of June 1718
This Bond was acknowledged in Court and admitted to record

p.   KNOW ALL MEN by these presents that wee GEORGE CHOWNING, THOMAS CHOW-
441   NING & JOHN OWEN are bound unto the Justices of Middlesex County in sum of
      two hundred pounds Sterling this 1st day of July 1718.
The Condition of this obligation is such that if George Chowning cause to be paid unto
HENRY NASH Orphan of JOHN NASH all Estate as appear to be due said Orphan as soon as
he shall attain to lawfull age and keep harmless the Justices from trouble about the
Estate that then this obligation to be void or else to remain
George Chowning
Thomas Chowning   John Owen
At a Court held for Middx. County the 3d day of July 1718
This bond was acknowledged & admitted to record

p.   KNOW ALL MEN by these presents that wee JAMES WALKER, JOHN ROBINSON,
442   BARTHOLOMEW YATES and WILLIAM STANARD of Middlesex County are bound
      unto our Sovereign Lord the King in sum of one thousand pounds Sterl. this 5th
day of August 1718.
The Condition of this obligation is such that Whereas James Walker is by virtue of a

Comission from the Honble ALEXANDER SPOTSWOOD His Majesties Lt. Governor & Commander in Cheif of the Dominion of Virginia appointed Sheriff of abovesaid County of Middx. for this ensueing year Now if said James Walker Sheriff shall render unto the Auditor a full account of all his Majesties Revenues and dues in said County also due payment make of all publick & County dues as shall be levied and that he diligently enquire & find out the true quantity of land held by any person and return a true list or rent role of same to his Majesties Auditor and full performance make of all things appertaining to the Office of Sheriff that then this obligation to be void or else to stand

                                James Walker   John Robinson
                                Bar: Yates   Wil. Stanard

At a Court held for Middx. County the 5th day of August 1718
This bond was presented in Court and acknowledged and admitted to record

pp.   KNOW ALL MEN by these presents that we MARY WARWICK Widow, CHARLES LEE
442-   & JOHN OWEN of Middlesex County are bound unto the Justices of the said County
443   in sum of three hundred pounds Sterl. this 5th day of August 1718.
        The Condtion of this obligation is such that if Mary Warwick Admx. of THOMAS WARWICK deced do make a perfect inventory of all the goods of the said deced and exhibit the same in the County Court as required and further do make a true account of her actings and doings therein when required and if it shall hereafter appear that any last Will and Testament was made by the said deced deliver up her Letters of Administration that then this obligation to be void otherwise to remain
In presence of THO: EDWARDS,   Mary *C^M* Warwick
    W. STANARD   Cha: Lee   John Owen 1718
At a Court held for Middx. County the 5th day of August 1718
This bond was acknowledged and admitted to record

p.   KNOW ALL MEN by these presents that wee ROBERT GEORGE JUNR. & ANNE his
443 Wife, ROBERT GEORGE and JOHN OWEN of County of Middlesex are bound unto the
    Justices of said County in sum of three hundred pounds Sterl. this 5th day of
August 1718.
  The Condition of this obligation is such that if Robert George and Anne his Wife Exectrs. of the last Will and Testamt. of ARTHUR NASH deced do make a true inventory of the said Estate & exhibit the same in County Court when required and do well and truly deliver all Legacys contained in said Testament that then this obligation to be void otherwise to remain
In presence of BAR: YATES   Robert George junr.
                             Anne George   Robert George *R*
                                John Owen
At a Court held for Middx. County the 5th day of August 1718
This bond was acknowledged and admitted to record

pp.   ALEXANDER SPOTSWOOD his Majestys Lieutenant Governour & Commander in
443- Chief of the Colony & Dominion of Virginia to JAMES WALKER Gent Greeting.
444   By Virtue of the power to me given as Commander in Chief of this Dominion I do appoint you to be Sheriff of the County of Middlesex dureing pleasure and that you be accordingly sworn as soon as may be and before you be sworn you enter into bond before the Justices in the penal sum of one thousand pounds Sterl. to render unto the Receiver General a full accompt of all his Majesties Revenue and dues in same County dureing term of your Sherivalty & also paymt. make of all publick dues as shall be levied and true performance make of all matters belonging to the office of the

Sheriff and I do hereby command all officers Civil & Military and all other his Majesties Subjects to be aiding & assisting to you as Sheriff. Given under my hand & seale of the Colony at Williamsburgh the fourteenth day of May 1718 in the fourth year of the Reign of our Sovereign Lord King George

                                                         A. SPOTSWOOD

p.   KNOW ALL MEN by these presents that we WILLIAM DAVIS, OLIVER SEGAR &
444   JAMES MEACHAM of the County of Middlesex are bound unto the Justices of the
        said County in sum of one hundred pounds Sterl. this second day of September
1718. The Condition of this obligation is such that if William Davis pay unto ANNE NASH
Orphan of JOHN NASH deced all estate due said Orphan as soon as she shall attain to
lawfull age and keep harmless said Justices from trouble about the Estate that then this
obligacon to be void or else to be
In presence of MATT. KEMP,   William Davis
        ROBT. GEORGE   Oliver Segar   James Meacham
    At a Court held for Middlesex County the 2d day of September 1718
This Bond was acknowledged and admitted to record

pp.   THIS INDENTURE made the Seven & twentieth day and eight & twentieth day of
444-   August 1718 Between ROBERT BIGG of ye County of Middlesex and ELIZABETH
446   his Wife of one part and MATTHEW KEMP of same County Whereas said Robert
        Bigg and Eliza. his Wife by Indenture dated the day before the date hereof did
sell unto Matthew Kemp Sixty acres of land being part of the plantation whereon the sd
Robert & Eliza. now live and bounded beginning at a marked tree standing on the East
side of ye mouth of Blands Creek & running paralell wth the Pattent of PEREGRIN
BLAND deced North by East until said Course meets with the head of ye Creek thence
down the said Creek to the beginning place which parcell of land was sold to JAMES
PATE Father of ye aforesaid ELIZABETH by Matthew Kemp deced ye Father of ye aforesaid Matthew Kemp party to these presents as by Deed dated thirtieth day of March 1695
and recorded in Middlesex Court the 1st day of April next and by the death of said James
Pate the land decended to the said Elizabeth (his only Daughter & heir) To Hold unto
Matthew Kemp to the intent that by virtue thereof and of the statute for transferring
uses into possession said Matthew Kemp might be in actuall possession Now This Indenture Witnesseth that Robert Bigg and Elizabeth his Wife for sume of one & twenty
pounds of Lawfull mony of Great Britain paid by Matthew Kemp do confirm unto ye said
Matthew Kemp the aforesaid land
    In presence of JOHN CURTIS,   Robert Bigg
        RICHD. DANIELL, EDWARD SMITH   Eliza S Bigg
    At a Court held for Middlesex County the second day of September 1718
Robert Bigg & Eliza. his Wife came into Court & acknowledged their lease and release to
Matthew Kemp the said Elizabeth being first examined which is admitted to record

pp.   TO ALL TO WHOM these presents shall come Know Ye that I the said OLIVER
446-   SEGAR for consideration of Sixty five pounds Sterl. & six hundred pounds of
447   Tobacco by WILLIAM GRAY paid do quit claim unto William Gray all demands
        which sd Oliver Seager ever had to a tract of land in Middlesex County which
was the fifth day November 1709 conveyed by Deed of Release from THOMAS DUDLEY
unto Oliver Seager and said William Gray in Jointenancy being the moiety or one half
part of three hundred acres of land which was by us the said Segar & Gray purchased of
Thomas Dudley In Witness I set my hand and seal this fifth day of August 1718

In presence of WM. GORDON,   Oliver Segar
    EDWIN THACKER, MATT. KEMP 1718
  At a Court held for Middlesex County the 2d day of September 1718
This Deed acknowledged & admitted to record
  KNOW ALL MEN by these presents that I Oliver Segar am bound unto William Gray in
the sum of one hundred and thirty pounds Sterl. this fifth day of August 1718.
  The Condition of this obligation is such that if Oliver Segar shall truely observe the
conditions in the release of land to William Gray that then this obligation to be void else
to remain
In presence of WM. GORDON,   Oliver Segar
    EDWIN THACKER
  At a Court held for Middx. County the second day of September 1718
This bond was acknowledged and admitted to record

pp.   THIS INDENTURE made the 7th October 1718 Between HANNAH MACKTYRE in
447- County of Middlesex & Parish of Christ Church of one part and GEORGE GOSS &
448 ELIZA. his Wife Witness that for ye full satisfaction to them in hand paid do ack-
    nowledge themselves satisfied have sould unto Hannah Macktyre one certain
ISLAND or peice of land lying in the Dragon Swamp commonly known by the name of
GOSSES ISLAND being bounded on ye upper side of it on RENOLS's line & on the lower
side on George Gosses line to contain the full breadth of his said Island from the main-
land to Great Run of ye Draggon Swamp
In presence of DAVID D GEORGE,   Geo: Goss
    JOS. HARDEE   Eliza. E Goss
  At a Court held for Middlesex County the 7th day of October 1718
George Goss came into Court and acknowledged this Deed to Hannah Macktyre which is
admitted to record and Eliza. Goss relinquished her right of Dower in said land which is
also recorded.
  KNOW ALL MEN by these presents that I George Goss and Eliza. my Wife am bound unto
Hannah Macktyre in sume of Forty pounds Sterl. money of England the 7th day of Octo-
ber 1718. The Condition of this obligation is such that if George Goss and Eliza. his Wife
shall at all times keep Hannah Macktyre from all trouble from the Deed of Saile for an
Island in the Draggon Swamp that then the above obligation to be void otherways to
stand
  In presence of DAVID D GEORGE,   Geo: Goss
    JOS. HARDEE   Eliza: E Goss
  At a Court held for Middx. County the 7th day of October 1718
This bond was acknowledged and admitted to record.

pp.   THIS INDENTURE made the sixth and seventh day of October 1718 between JOSEPH
448- GOARE of the Parish of Christ Church in the County of Middlesex Planter of one
450 part and JOHN GRYMES of same Planter Witnesseth that said Joseph Goare for
    sum of Five pounds currant money doth sell unto sd John Grymes five acres in
Middlesex County where said Joseph Goare now liveth and whereof he is now seised in
fee simple by Will decent from JOHN GOARE deceased to whom the same was granted by
a Patent dated the 24th of May 1664 and bounded beginning at a red oak standing at the
head of a branch and from thence runing down the courses of said branch to a Maple
from thence West into the Great Swamp comonly called Gardiners Swamp till it meets
with a line of Mr. Grymes own land all which land now in actuall possession of said
John Grymes by Virtue of a sale for the term of six months and the force of the Statute

for transferring uses into possession
In presence of MATT: KEMP,   Joseph Goare
     WIL. STANARD, JNO. CURTIS
     At a Court held for Middx. County the 4th of November 1718
Joseph Goare came into Court and acknowledged his lease and release which is admitted
to record & LUCRETIA GOARE also appeared in Court and relinquished her right of
Dower wch is also admitted to record
     KNOW ALL MEN by these presents that I Joseph Goare am bound unto John Grymes in
sum of Fifty pounds Currt. money this seventh day of October 1718.
     The Condition of this obligation is such that if Joseph Goare keep all articles in Inden-
ture which he ought to keep that then this obligacon to be void otherwise to remain
In presence of MATT KEMP,   Joseph Goare
     WIL. STANARD, JNO. CURTIS
     At a Court held for Middx. County the 4th day of November 1718
This Bond was acknowledged & admitted to record

pp.   THIS INDENTURE made the tenth and eleventh day of October 1718 Between
450-   ROBERT DUDLEY of the Parish of Christ Church in County of Middlesex of one
452   part and AUGUSTIN SMITH of Parish of Petso in County of GLOUCESTER Witnes-
         seth that said Robert Dudley did grant unto Augustin Smith land containing One
hundred acres in Parish of Christ Church and County of Middlesex begining at a
marked tree by Peyanketack River side and running North East to a marked tree of
PHILIP TORKSEYs land from thence Northwest to the River then down the River to the
place it began which said land is part of a Patent of Six hundred and fifty acres granted
unto AUGUSTIN MOORE dated the 29th of June 1652 and sold by said Augustin Moore unto
JOHN SCARBROUGH the Father unto John Scarbrough who sold this land unto Major
ROBERT DUDLEY Father to the within menconed Robert Dudley To Hold the said land for
six months to the end that by vertue thereof and the statute for transferring uses into
possession said Augutin Smith might be in actuall possession Now this Indenture Wit-
nesseth tht said Robert Dudley for sum of Sixty seven pounds lawfull money Sterl. paid
hath released unto said Augustine Smith his heires same lying adjoyning unto the
North side of Peyanketank River
In presence of us. JOHN ✝ DUDLEY SENR.,   Robert Dudley
     WILLIAM W CAIN, JOHN ✝ DUDLEY JUNR.
     At a Court held for Middlesex County the 4th day of November 1718
Robert Dudley acknowledged this lease and release which is admitted to record ELIZA-
BETH DUDLEY Wife of said Robert Dudley came into Court and acknowledged her relin-
quishment of Dower in the land conveyed to sd Augustine Smith gentl. which is also
admitted to record.

p.   KNOW ALL MEN by these presents that we JAMES WALKER, JOHN PRICE &
452   HARRY BEVERLEY are bound unto our Sovereign Lord the King in sum of twenty
         nine thousand one hundred and Sixty eight pounds of good sweet scented
Tobacco this fourth day of November 1718.
     The Condition of this obligation is such that if James Walker Sheriff shall truly collect
the publick and County levys put into his hands and faithfully pay all the said publick
levys unto the Creditors for whom they are raised as directed by an Act of Assembly
made at a Generall Assembly begun at his Majts. Royall Capitol the 23d day of October in
the Fourth year of the Reign of her late Majesty Queen Anne 1705 Intituled an Act concerning the Publick & County Leveys that then this obligation to be void or else to stand

In presence of us JOHN CURTIS,   Ja: Walker
        THOS. EDWARD   Harry Beverley   John Price
    At a Court held for Middlesex County the 4th day of November 1718
This bond was acknowledged and admitted to record

p.   Middlesex County Sct. JOSEPH WILLIS aged about twenty five years was this day
453   brought before me on suspicion of having stolen some things from Collo.
        NICHOLAS SMITH of the County of RICHMOND & particularly a Silver Spoon upon
examination he the said Joseph produced part of silver spoon (the hand being half
brooke of) which he said he bought from JAMAICA, but Mrs. ELIZA. BEVERLEY (Wife of
Mr. HARRY BEVERLEY) being present challenged the spoon and said it belonged to her
& she produced a spoon exactly like it (as much as there was of it) at last I ordered him
to be searched & found upon him the other part of the handle of the Spoon (which he
denied to have had before) and compared it with Mrs. Beverleys & found it directly like
both in make & Cypher after this he confessed that he the said Joseph Willis did take the
above menconed spoone out of the porch of Mr. Beverleys house and being asked what
made him break it he said could not tell this done before me JOHN ROBINSON one of his
Majts. Justices of the peace for this County this 25th day of October 1718
·Test JA: WALKER.   Joh: Robinson
  Middlesex County Sct (Willis Mittimus) I herewith send you the body of JOSEPH WILLIS
who was this day brought before me on suspicion of felony and hath confessed the fact
before me on Examinacon. You are therefore him in your Goal safely to keep till he
shall be thence delivered by due course of Law. Given under my hand this 25th day of
October 1718.
To the Sheriff of Middlesex County   Joh: Robinson

pp.   THIS INDENTURE made the second day of December 1718 Between THOMAS
453-   MOUNTAGUE and GRACE his Wife of County of Middlesex of one part and ROBERT
456   GALLBREATH of same County Witnesseth that said Thomas Mountague & Grace
        his Wife for sum of five shillings lawfull money Sterl. doth sell unto said Robert
Gallbreath all that parcell of land commonly called MICKLEBURROUGH PLANTATION in
Middlesex County containing One hundred and ten acres of land and bounded begining
at the mouth of a Swamp commonly known by the name of JOHN ALICE's Swamp &
runing the severall turnings of said Swamp up to the head thereof that makes towards
JOHN SOUTHARDs & THOMAS CRANK to a marked white oak & a small Gum standing at the
head of the valey the line of John Southards which was formerly the line of RICHD.
WHITE and JOHN WELCH then South West along line to the White Marsh then along the
White Marsh southeast to the land of OBERT now in possession of JAMES CURTIS JUNR.
thence Northeast down a small branch to a Swamp that parts the said land and land of
James Curtis Junr. then down the said Swamp to the Creek side then up said Creek to the
beginning place all which land is in the Parish of Christ Church in County of Middlesex
and now in the occupation of said Robert Gallbreath To Hold unto said Robert Gallbreath the term of six months to the end that by virtue of the Statute for transferring
uses into possession he may be in actuall possession Now This Indenture Witnesseth
that said Thomas Mountague and Grace his Wife for sum of Eighty pounds Current
money doth confirm unto said Robert Gallbreath all the aforesaid tract of land
In presents of WILLIAM GRAY,   Thos. Mountague
        WILLIAM DAVIS, HUMPHREY JONES   Grace ⊊ Mountague
    At a Court held for Middlesex County the 2d day of December 1718
Thomas Mountague Junr. & Grace his Wife came into Court and acknowledged this their

lease and release to Robert Galbreath (the said Grace being first privately examined) which is admitted to record.

KNOW ALL MEN by these presents that I Thomas Mountague Junr. of County of Middlesex am bound unto Robert Galbreath in sum of one hundred and sixty pounds Currt. money this second day of December 1718.

The Condition of this obligation is such that if Thomas Mountague his heires shall at all time keep all agreements contained in Indenture of lease and release which ought to be fullfilled that then this obligacon to be void otherwise to remain

In presents of WILLIAM GRAY,   Thos: Mountague junr.
    WILLIAM DAVIS, HUMP: JONES

At a Court held for Middlesex County the 2d day of December 1718
Thomas Mountague junr. appd. in Court & acknowledged his bond which is admitted to record

p.   KNOW ALL MEN by these presents that I GEORGE CHOWNING of LANCASTER
456   COUNTY Planter stand indebted unto WILLIAM GORDON of Middlesex County Mer-
         cht. in sum of three hundred pounds Sterl. this 9th day of September 1718.

The Condition of this obligation is such that if George Chowning shall by Deed convey his remaining part of a tract of land lying betwixt Robinson Mill Creek and Morgans Creek according to THOMAS CHOWNINGs Patten of sd land which is Three hundred and fifty acres unto the said William Gordon to be acknowledged in the Middlesex County Court by the 20th of October next without fraud that then this obligacon to be void or to stand

In presence of CHRISTOPHER ɤ STEVENS   George Chowning
    THO: Mc: CLELLAND

At a Court held for Middlesex County the 2d day of December 1718
This bond was admitted to record

pp.   Mr. GEORGE CHOWNING Account Currant Dr. 1709 To sundry goods sold him this
456-   day particulars in Joyrnal No. 1 Fol. 21; to his Bill on me payable JOHN PYNES;
457   to do. assigned JAMES WILSON 1710 to do. pd Collo. WM. CHURCHILL, to Cr. given
         Doctr. JOHN KNIGHT p his order. 1711/12. To do. to HENRY TOWLES, to Credit
given THOMAS MARSHALL, to Sundry goods to said Chowning this day; to Credit given HENRY TOWLES, to paid Collo. CORBINs Judgmt agst sd Chowning. 1712 To cash lent him. 1713 To sundry goods sold him; to my Draught on MR. WORMELEY to sd Chowning; to cash paid Mr. OLIVER SEGAR for him; to his draught on me to pay JOHN PYNES. 1713/14 To cash lent him. 1714. To the ballance of ISAAC BATEMANs Acct; to Cr. given Capt BENJAMIN GRAVES p sd Chownings Order. 1715 To his Bill on me payable sd Graves.

Contra is March 1709/10. By 400 acres of land bot of him as p Deeds of Conveyance. Sept 9th 1712 by 350 acres more as p bond of Assurance for conveying to me. By the Ballance of the acct. Currt. charged p Cort. made up the 7th of September 1713. 27..19..10
                         Errors excepted p   WM. GORDON

At a Court held for Middlesex County the 2d day of December 1718
William Gordon produced the within acct. between him and George Chowning deced and made oath thereto MARY late Wife of the said George also appeared in Court and made oath that she heard her sd husband a day before his death say that Mr. Gordon owed him ten or twelve pounds on ballance of his acct. which is hereby certifyed and at sd Gordons motion the said Acct. is admitted to record.

pp.   KNOW ALL MEN by these presents that we RICHARD ALLEN, JOHN PRICE & ED-
457-   MUND MICKLEBURROUGH are bound unto the Justices of Middlesex County in
458   sum of two hundred pounds Sterl. this 2d day of December 1718.
        The Condition of this obligation is such that if Richard Allen truly pay unto
JOHN ALLEN Orphan of Richard Allen deced all estates as appear due to sd Orphan as
soon as he shall attain to lawfull age that then the above obligacon to be void or else to
remain.
In presents of us THOS. EDWARDS,   Richd. *a* Allen
        W. STANARD   John Price   Edmund Mickleburrough
    At a Court held for Middlesex County the 2d day of December 1718
This bond was acknowledged in Court and admitted to record

pp.   THIS INDENTURE made the second and third day of November in the year 1719
458-   between JOHN BRADLEY of County of Middlesex of one part and ARMISTEAD
460   CHURCHHILL of same Witnesseth that for sum of Forty five pounds Sterling to
        said John Bradley paid he hath sold unto Armistead Churchhill in his possession
being by virtue of sale to him made for one year all that land containing One hundred
acres purchased by said John Bradley of WILLIAM SANDIFORD and FRANCES his Wife &
bounded on the lands of HENRY ARMISTED, RICHARD STEEVENS and the sd Armistead
Churchhill as by records of sd County Court being dated the second day of October as by
records of said County Court made between sd William Sandiford and Frances his Wife of
one part and sd John Bradley dated the second day of October 1715
In presence of DANIEL SWINEY,   Jno. Bradley
        THO: EDWARDS
    At a Court held for Middlesex County the third day of November 1719
John Bradley came into Court and acknowledged his lease and release which is admitted
to record
    KNOW ALL MEN by these presents that I MARY BRADLEY Wife of John Bradley do
freely relinquish my right of Dower unto lands conveyd by my husband to Armistead
Churchill and depute Thomas Edwards of the aforesd County to acknowledge my relinqt.
for me in Middlesex County Court. In Witness I have set my hand and seal this third day
of November 1719.
In presence of JOHN READ,   Mary /M\ Bradley
        WILLIAM W HACKNEY
    At a Court held for Middlesex County the 3d day of November 1719
This Letter of Attorney was proved in Court and admitted to record

pp.   KNOW ALL MEN by these presents that wee JAMES LEWIS and CHRISTOPHER KIL-
460-   BEY of Middx. County are bound unto the Justices of said County in sum of one
461   hundred pounds Sterl. this 30th day of ( ) 1718.
        The Condition of this obligation is such that if James Lewis do well and truely
pay unto KATHI KILBEY Orphan of WILL: KILBEY deced all Estate as shall appear to be
due sd Orphan as soon as she shall attain to lawfull age and keep harmless the Justices
from all trouble about the Estate that then this obligation to be void or else to remain
In presents of us   THOS. EDWARDS,   James Lewis
        H. THACKER   Christopher Kilbey
    Acknowledged in Court the 3d day of Janry 1718 and admitted to record

p.   KNOW ALL MEN by these presents that I MATHEW KEMP of Middx. County and
461   Parrish of Christ Church for a valuable consideration have sold unto MATTHEW
        HILLIARD one negro boy named Billy that I said Mathew Kemp doe warrant unto

sd <u>MARTHA HELLARD her</u> heirs for ever as Wittness my hand this 19th Septr. 1707.
In presence of ROGER JONES.   Matt. Kemp
    ROBERT Ᵽ UMPHRES
At a Court held for Middlesex County the 3d day of January 1718
At the motion of DUDLEY JOLLEY this Deed was admitted to record

p.   KNOW ALL MEN by these presents that we ROBERT DUDLEY and THOMAS MACHEN
462   of Middlesex County are bound unto the Justices of above County in sum of fifty
    pounds Sterling this 3d day of March 1718.
The Condition of this obligation is such that if Robert Dudley Admr. of the Will anexed
of ELIZA. ELLIOT Widow deced doe make a true Inventory of said Estate and truely ad-
minister according to Law that then this obligation to be voyd otherwise to remain
In presence of THOS: EDWARDS,   Robert Dudley
                                      Thos. Machen
  At a Court held for Middx County the 3d day of March 1718
This bond was acknowledged and admitted to record

pp.   KNOW ALL MEN by these presents that wee ELIZABETH CRANK, THOMAS CHOW-
463-   NING and JOHN CHOWNING of Middlesex County are bound unto the Justices of the
464   said County in sum of two hundred pounds Sterling this 3d day of March 1718.
      The Condition of this obligation is such that if Elizabeth Crank Exer. of the last
Will and Testament of MATTW. CRANK deced do make a true inventory of said estate and
cause the same to be exhibited in the County Court when required and do make a just
account of her actings and doings therein that then this obligation to be voyd
otherwise to be
In presence of ZACH: LEWIS   Eliza. Crank
                         Thos: Chawing   John Chawing
  At a Court held for Middlesex County the 3d day of March 1718
This Bond was acknowledged and admitted to record

pp.   At a Court held for Middlesex County the 9th day of March 1718
464   Upon the Petition of EDWIN THACKER Gent it is ordered that Capt. ROBERT DANIEL
465   JAMES MEACHAM and JOHN ALLDING or any two of them some time between this
    and next Court meet on the land belonging to the Orphans of JOHN NASH deced
lying on the North side of the southermost maine branch of Sunderland Creek opposite
to the MILL lately called by name of ROBINSONS MILL in this County and there to vallue
one acre of land to build a Mill according to Law and the prayer of the Petitioner and
report proceedings to the next Court.   Copia Wm. Stanard
  At a Court held for Middlesex County the 17th day of April 1719
Robert Daniel, James Meacham and John Alldin being appointed by the last Court to
view and value an acre of land belonging to the Orphans of John Nash deced for Mr.
EDWIN THACKER to build a Mill upon not haveing made their report the sd Order to con-
tinue till next Court and ordered that is be performed according to the said Order
  Middx. County In Obedience to the above order we the Subscribers did meet on the
land belonging to the Orphans of John Nash and have viewed one acre there for which
is bounded as followeth begining at a red oak by the side of the old Mill Pond from
thence to a White oak by the ROAD SIDE thence to a Gum by the Run side thence to the
be to the beginning which sd Acre of land wee have valued at ten shillings. Given
under our hand the day above said   Robert Daniel
                             James Meacham   John Alldin

At a Court held for Middlesex County the 7th day of July 1719
The within report was admitted to record

p.
465
To the Worshipfull Court. EDWIN THACKER Humbly pleaseth That he is willing and desirous to build a WATER GRIST MILL on the Southermost branch of Sunderland Creek in this County and that he hath land on one side the sd run thereof and forasmuch as the land on the other side belongs to persons under age, who are not able to make him a sale of an acre for ye use the Plt. therefore humbly prays that your Worships will appoint to such persons as you shall think fitt to view the sd land and vallue an acre thereof and that the Plt. be put in possession wth the same as the Law directs and he shall pray etc.

pp.
465-
466
KNOW ALL MEN by these presents that wee GEORGE BERRICK and MATT. KEMP are bound unto the Justices of Middlesex County in the sum of Fifty pounds Sterling this 3d day of March 1718/9.
    The condition of this obligation is such that if George Berrick do pay unto MARGARETT HAINES Orphan of CHARLES HAINES deced all such estate as appear due to sd Orphan as she shall attaine to lawfull age and keep harmless said Justices from all trouble about the Estate that then the above obligation to be voyd or to remain
In presence of THOS. EDWARDS,   Geo: Berrick
    JOHN OWEN   1718/9   Matt Kemp
  At a Court held for Middx. County the 3d day of March 1718
This bond was acknowledged and admitted to record

pp.
467-
468
KNOW ALL MEN by these presents that wee JUDITH TRIGG, HENRY BESKET, THOMAS KIDD and THOMS. HACKETT are bound unto the Justices of Middlesex County in the sum of two hundred pounds Sterling this 7th day April 1719.
    The Condition of this obligation is such that if Judith Trigg Administratrix of ABRAHAM TRIGG deced cause to make a perfect inventory and exhibit the same in the County Court when required and truely administer according to Law and if it appear hereafter that any last Will and Testament was made by said deced that said Administratrix being required deliver up her Letters of Administration that then this obligation to be voyd else to remain in full force
                            Judith T Trigg   Henry Besket
                            Thomas Kidd   Thoms. Hackett
  At a Court held for Middx. County the 7th day of April 1719
This bond was acknowledged and admitted to record

pp.
468-
469
KNOW ALL MEN by these presents that wee WILLIAM WOOD and MATTHEW HUNT are bound unto our Sovereign Lord King George in sum of Ten thousand pounds of Tobo: this 7th day of Apl. 1719.
    The Condition of this obligation is such that Whereas Wm. Wood hath obtained a lycense to keep an ORDINARY at his house in URBANNA Now if said Wm. Wood doth provide in his sd Ordinary cleanly lodgeing and Dyett for travellers and stableage fodder and provender or pasturage as the seasons may require for their horses for term of one year from 7th of April 1719 and not suffer any unlawfull gaming nor on the Sabbath any to drink more then necessary that then this obligation to be voyd otherwise to remain
In presence of ROBERT BEVERLEY,   Wil. Wood
                                                          Matt: Hunt

At a Court held for Middlesex County the 7th day of April 1719
This bond was acknowledged & admitted to record

pp.   THIS INDENTURE made this Sixth and Seventh day of Apl. 1719 Between THOMAS
469-   MOUNTAGUE JUNR. of County of Middx. Plantr: of one part and WM. SEGAR of the
474   same County Planter Witnesseth that sd Thomas Mountague for sum of Sixty
         pounds Sterling mony of great Brittain doth sell unto Wm. Segar all that one
hundred acres of land in Christ Church Parish in County of Middlesex begining at a
marked Willow tree at the head of a branch near the line that parts this land from
CHAMLETT and Segars land runing thence down the aforesaid Branch it severall
courses untill it meets with a Creek called Sandy Point Creek alias Muddy Creek thence
down ye sd Creek several courses to a white oak on a point on the South side of the sd
Creek it being the begining place of a Patent of land for One thousand acres of land
granted lately to PETER MOUNTAGUE by pattent dated the 24th day of Octr. 1701 and
runing thence South West to the first beginning place all which premises are in
actuall possession of said William Segar by Virtue of Indenture for one year and by virtue of the statute for transferring uses into possession
In presence of WIL. STANARD,   Thomas Mountague
      ZACHRY LEWIS, RICHARD DANIEL
   At a Court held for Middx. County the 7th day of April 1719
Thomas Mountague Jur. came into Court and acknowledged his lease and release of land
to William Segar which is admitted to record

pp.   THIS INDENTURE made the Sixth and Seventh day of Aprill in the fifth year of
475-   reign of our Sovereign Lord George 1719 Between MARY HUTCHESON of the
480   County of ESSEX Widdow one of the Daughters and Coheires of WILLIAM NEEDLES
         late of County of Middlesex of one part and HENRY GILPIN of same County of
Middx. of other part Witnesseth that for sum of Twenty five pounds lawfull money of
great Britain hath sold unto Henry Gilpin in his actuall possession by force of sale to
him made for one whole year and Statute for transferring uses into possession all that
parcell of land bequeathed to sd WILLIAM NEADLES by JOHN NEEDLES his Father by his
last Will and Testmt. dated the six and twentieth day of May 1686 and which is now decended unto said Mary Hutcheson and FRANCIS the Wife of one WILLIAM HILL of the sd
County of Middlesex the only surviveing Daughters and Coheires of sd William Needles
In presence of WM. JOHNSON,   Mary ✗ Hutcheson
      THOMAS EDWARDS
   At a Court held for Middlesex County the 7th day of April 1719
Mary Hutcheson acknowledged this lease and release to Henry Gilpin which is admitted
to record

p.   KNOW ALL MEN by these presents that wee RICHARD DANIEL, JOHN SMITH and
480   JOHN MURRY are bound unto our Sovereign Lord George in the sum of ten
         thousand pounds of Tobo: this 7th day of Aprill 1719.
   The Condition of this obligation is such that Whereas Richard Daniel hath obtained a
Lysence to keep and ORDINARY at his House in this County Now if said Richard Daniel
shall constantly provide good and cleanly lodgeing and dyett for Travillers and stableage fodder and provender or pasturage as the seasons require for their horses for term
of one year from 7th of Apl. & shall not suffer any unlawfull gameing nor on the
Sabbath day suffer any to drink more than is necessary that then this obligation to be
void otherwise to remain

Richd. Daniell
John Smith   John Murry

At a Court held for Middx.County the 7th day of April 1719
This bond was presented in Court and admitted to record

p.   TO ALL TO WHOM these presents shall come I MARTHA GARDNER for love I do
481   bare my loveing Son THOMAS HILLIARD hath given one negro boy named Billy
          a feather bed and boulster one small iron pot To Hold without any maner of con-
dition In Witness I have set my hand & seal this fifth day of December in the second
year of Reign of our Sovereign Lord George in year 1715
In presents off THOMAS SMITH,   Martha /M Gardiner
        FRANS. HILL, JOHN & GIBS
At a Court held for Middx. County the 5th day of May 1718
John Gibs made oath that he saw Martha Gardiner sign & deliver the above Deed and on
the said Gibs motion on behalf of Thomas Hyleard the sd Deed is admitted to record

p.   KNOW ALL MEN by these presents that we JOHN VIVION, EDWIN THACKER & WM.
482   STANARD are bound unto our Sovereign Lord the King in sum of one thousand
          pounds Sterling this 2d day of June 1719.
The Condition of this obligation is such that Whereas John Vivion is by Comission from
the Honble ALEXANDER SPOTSWOOD appointed Sheriff for this ensueing year Now if sd
John Vivion shall at all times render unto the Auditor a perfect account of all his
Majtys revenues and dues in sd County and execute all warrants which shall come from
the Lieut. Govenr. or any of the Councill of State and deligently inquire and find out
the true quantity of land held in said County and return a perfect rent roll of the same
to his Majtys Auditor that then this obligation to be void or else to stand
                                                       John Vivion
                                        Edwin Thacker   Wil. Stanard
At a Court held for Middlesex County the 2d day of June 1719
This bond was presented in Court and admitted to record

pp.   KNOW ALL MEN by these presents that wee KATHARINE WARRICK, JOHN OWEN
483-   and JAMES BRISTOW are bound unto Mr. ROGER JONES gent first in comission of
484   the peace for County of Middlesex in sum of three hundred pounds this 2d day of
          June 1719.
The Condition of this obligation is such that if Katherine Warrick Executrix of the last
Will and Testament of PHILLIP WARRICK deced do make a true inventory of all the
deced Estate and exhibit the same in County Court as required and do make Acct. of her
actings and doings therein and pay all the Legacies contained in sd Testament that then
this obligation to be voyd otherwise to remain
In presence of ROBERT BEVERLEY,   Katherine /K Warrick
        JOHN CURTIS   John Owen   James Bristow
At a Court held for Middx. County the 2d day of June 1719
This bond was acknowledged and admitted to record

pp.   KNOW ALL MEN by these presents that wee ABIGAL CHILTON, THOMAS CHILTON
484-   and ZEBULON CHILTON of Middlesex County are bound unto ROGER JONES gent
485   first in Comission of the peace for said County in sum of one hundred pounds
          Sterl. this 2d day of June 1719.
The Condition of this obligation is such that if Abigal Chilton Executrix of the last Will
and Testament of PETER CHILTON deced do make a true Inventory of said deced Estate and

exhibit the same in County Court when required and truly administer according to Law and make a true account of her actings and doings therein and truly pay all the Legacys that then this obligation to be voyd otherwise to remain

Abigal ⁊ Chilton

Thos. ᴍ Chilton   Zebulon Ħ Chilton

At a Court held for Middlesex County the 2d day of June 1719
This bond was presented in Court and admitted to record

pp. THIS INDENTURE made the 31st day of July 1719 Between THOMAS KIDD of County
486- of Middx. and ALICE his Wife of one part and ROBERT DANIEL of same County
488 gent Witnesseth that said Thomas Kidd and Alice Kidd for Ten shillings sell unto
Robert Daniell one acre of land in County of Middlesex and bounded half an acre
part whereof lyeing on the North side of the White Oake Swamp at the end of sd Robert
Daniels Mill Dam joyning in NICHOLAS BRISTOWs line and the other halfe acre part
lying on the side of the sd Swamp at the other end of the sd Dam binding on ROBERT
BLACKLYs line the sd halfe acre being bound Round with marked trees now in the
actuall possession of sd Robert Daniel
In presence of us JON. OWEN,   ‾   Thos. Kidd
   · ROBERT DANIELL, THOMAS Ⱶ KIDD JUNR.   Alice ℓ Kidd
At a Court held for Middx. County the 7th day of August 1719
Thomas Kidd came into Court and acknowledged the above Deed and it was admitted to
record Alice also ye Wife of sd Thomas relinquished her Dower in the land which is also
recorded

p. MEMORANDUM that according to an Order of Middlesex County Court dated the
488 third day of March full seizen of the sd acre of land was delivered by Mr. ROBERT
DANIELL, Mr. JOHN ALLDIN and Mr. JAMES MEACHAM viewers and appraisers in
sd Order appointed to EDWIN THACKER by Turf and Twigg in presence of
ROGER ⱹPRTICHETT   CHARLES ✗ COOPER
At a Court held for Middx. County the 4th day of August 1719
On the motion of Edwin Thacker the above livery of Seizin admitted to record

pp. THIS INDENTURE made the nineteenth day of August 1719 Between JOHN GUT-
489- TREY of County of Middlesex and JANE his Wife of one part and ROBERT DANIELL
491 of same County Witnesseth that sd John and Jeane Guttry for fifty shillings Cur-
rent money have sold unto sd Robert Daniell two acres of land in County of
Middx. bounded lying on the side of the Bryers Swamp bounded with the land of one
KATHERINE YOUNG Widow and Bryers Swamp and line of marked trees running from
the sd Bryers Swamp to the line of sd Katherine Young adjoining upon the land of sd
John Guttrey now in actuall possession of sd Robt. Daniel
In presence of WM. GARWOOD,   John Ⱶ⁻⁻Ⱶ Guttrey
   JOHN REIGON, JOHN HUNT   Jane Ɨ Guttrey
At a Court held for Middlesex County the 7th day of Septr. 1719
John Guttrey and Jane his Wife acknowledged their Deed to Robert Daniell Junr. Jane
also the Wife of said John relinquished her dower in said land wch is add. to record

pp. THIS INDENTURE made the Eleventh and Twelfth day of June 1719 Between
491- ROBERT DUDLEY of County of Middlesex Gent. of one part and RICHD. BUCKNER of
498 County of ESSEX Gent of other part Witnesseth that said Robert Dudley for sum of
three hundred and fifty pounds Sterling do release unto sd Richd. Buckner now
in sd Richd. Buckner actuall possession by virute of sale and of the Statute for the

transferring of uses into possession being by Estimation Four hundred and fifty acres of land being part of Estate of Six hundred and fifty acres of land granted unto AUGUS-TINE MOORE Three hundred and fifty acres part of the sd Four hundred and fifty acres bequeathed by Col. RICHD. DUDLEY now deced to the sd Roberts Father by Deed of Gift and by Will and the other hundred acres of land purchased by sd Robert Father of Robert Dudley of one DANIEL RICE & conveyed to sd Robert Dudley Father to aforesd Robert party to these presents by Mr. JOHN GRYMES in behalfe of the sd Daniel Rice

In presence of THOMAS T HUBBART,   Robt. Dudley
    NICHOLAS N HAWKINS, JOHN I DAVIS,
    JAMES ROY

At a Court held for Middlesex County the first day of 7ber 1719

Robert Dudley came into Court and acknowledged his lease and release to Richard Buckner which is admitted to record ELIZABETH the Wife of said Robert came into Court and relinquished her dower in said land which is also admitted to record

KNOW ALL MEN by these presents that I Robert Dudley am bound unto Richard Buckner in sum of seven hundred pounds Sterling this 12th day of June 1719.

The Condition of this obligation is such that if Robert Dudley truely observe all the Covenants mentioned in Indentures and if Elizabeth Dudley Wife of said Robert shall relinquish her right of Dower that then this obligation to be void or remain in full force

In presence of THOMAS T HUBBART,   Robt. Dudley
    NICHOLAS N HAWKINS, JOHN I DAVIS,
    JAMES ROY

At a Court held for Middlesex County the 1st day of September 1719

Robert Dudley acknowledged the within bond which is admitted to record

p. 498   KNOW ALL MEN by these presents that we WILLIAM CARDWLL, THOMAS KID & THOMAS KID JUNR. are bound unto the Justices of Middlesex County in the sum of two hundred pounds Sterl. this 1st day of September 1719.

The Condition of this obligation is such that if William Cardwell shall truely pay unto MARY GOODRICH Orphan of JOHN GOODRICH deced all estate that shall appear to be due to said Orpan as soon as she shall attaine to lawfull age that then this obligation to be void else to be

In presence of JOHN VIVION   William W Cardwell
                                                        Thomas   Kidd junr.

At a Court held for Middx. County the 1st day of Sept. 1719

This bond was presented in Court and acknd. which is admitted to record

p. 499   KNOW ALL MEN by these presents that ROBERT DUDLEY of County of Middlesex am bound unto JOSEPH GOARE in the penall summe of one hundred pounds Sterling money of England this 7th day of November 1702.

The Condition of this obligation is such that if Robert Dudley let my Sister ELIZABETH DUDLEY have the two negro children she now hath the one named Morselles and the other Rose and Seven Golde Ringes with all her waring apparell and the Trunks that they are in and the Chest of Drawers to be free and at her own disposall when it shall please Almighty God to take her out of this world or when she pleases that then this obligation to be void or else to stand

In presence of us THOMAS MARSTON,   Robert R Dudley
    EDW. COUCH

At a Court held for Middlesex County the 3d day of November 1719

The within written bond was proved in Court to be the act & deed of Robert Dudley deced by the oath of Edward Couch & it was admitted to record

pp.   KNOW ALL MEN by these presents that I HENRY GILPIN Bricklayer of County of
499-   Middlesex am bound unto WILLIAM HILL Planter in penall sume of Eighty
500   pounds of good & lawfull money of England this twenty six day of Octobr: 1719.
        The Condition of this obligation is such that if Henry Gilpin at all times at re-
quest of said William Hill faithfully acknowledge all their claim of ye Plantation or
parcill of land commonly called by names JOHN HUGHSES and formerly belonging to
JOHN NEEDLES SENR. lying upon the Shell Neck Branche unto William Hill his heirs that
then this obligation to be void otherwise to stand
In presence of us GEORGE HARDIN,   Henry Gilpin
        JNO. JOHNSON
    At a Court held for Middx. County the 3d day of November 1719
Henry Gilpin came into Court and acknowledged his bond and it was admitted to record

p.   KNOW ALL MEN by these presents that I WILLIAM HILL planter of Middlesex am
500   bound unto HENRY GILPIN Bricklayer in the penall sum of Eighty pounds of
    good & lawfull money of England this twenty six day of Octobr: 1719.
The Condition of this obligation is such that if William Hill shall at all times at request
of Henry Gilpin truly acknowledge all claim to a plantation & dividend of land commonly called & known by name of the RICH NECK in County aforesaid being ajacent to
Penketank River formerly belonging to WILLIAM NEEDLES that then this present obligation to be void otherwise to stand
In presence of GEORGE HARDIN,   William *W* Hill
        JOHN JOHNSON
    At a Court held for Middx. County the 3d day of November 1719
William Hill acknowledged this bond which was admitted to record

pp.   TO ALL PEOPLE I JOHN SMITH of Parish of Christ Church in County of Middlesex
500-   in consideration of the love which I bear unto my well beloved Son THOS:
501   SMITH have granted unto said Thomas Smith his heirs forever that plantation of
    lands whereon he now dwells containing Two hundred acres of land in Parish of
Christ Church & County of Middlesex and now in occupation of said Thos: Smith. In Witness I sett my hand & seale this second day of Feby: in fifth yeare of the reign of our
Sovereign Lord George 1719
                            John Smith
    At a Court held for Middlesex County the 2d day of February 1719
John Smith came into Court and acknowledged his Deed to his Son which is admitted to
record.

pp.   THIS INDENTURE made the 7th day of December 1719 Between THOMAS CHEDLE of
501-   County of Middlesex & FRANCES his Wife of one part and JOSEPH HARDEE of the
503   same County Witnesseth that said Thos. Chedle and Frances his Wife for sum of
    thirteen pounds Sterling hath sold unto said Joseph Hardee his heires forever
fifty acres of land in Middlesex County being a parcell of land John Chedle decest purchased of WILLIAM WOODS and said Woods of Mr. ROBT. PRICE deced and joyning upon
the land of JNO. BLUFORD and DAVID GEORGE to begin at a Hickory in said John Blufords
line and to run Eastward across the neck by two trees such course as shall include the
said fifty acres of land
In presence of us JOHN OWEN 1719   Thomas Chedle
        DAVID D GEORGE, JANE X HARDY   Frances Ø Chedle

At a Court held for Middlesex County the 1st day of March 1719
Thomas Chedle came into Court and acknowledged the above Deed and it was admitted to
record FRANCES CHEDLE the Wife of said Thomas appeared and acknowledged her relinquishment of dower in the land and it is also recorded

pp.   KNOW ALL MEN by these presents that wee MANN PAGE & JOHN WORMELEY
503-   Acting Exers. of the last Will and Testament of ELIZABETH CHURCHHILL relict
504   and Executrix of the last Will and Testament of WILLIAM CHURCHHILL Esqr. late
       of County of Middlesex deced have appointed MATTHEW KEMP of County of Mid-
dlesex our Attorney to receive all sums of money goods & effects due to sd Estate and to
perform all things that shall be necessary about the premises we will ratify & allow as
fully as if we were present. In Witness whereof we have set our hands and seals this
Sixth day of July 1720
In presence of J. PRATT,   Mann Page
     EMANUEL JONES, BAYLEY KENT,   John Wormeley
     THOS. EDWARDS
   At a Court held for LANCASTER COUNTY the 13th day of July 1720
This Letter of Attorney was this day proved in open Court & by the oath of Bayley Kent
one of the witnesses thereto which is hereby certified
                             p   WM. DALE ClCur
   At a Court held for Middlesex County the 3d day of August 1720
This letter of Attorney proved by oath of Jno. Pratt another of the witnesses and
admitted to record

pp.   KNOW ALL MEN by these presents that I THOMAS CHEDLE and FRANCES his Wife
504-   in Parish of Christ Church County of Middlesex do bind ourselves to be paid unto
505   JOSEPH HARDEE the sum of five hundred pounds Sterling money of England this
       7th day of December 1719.
   The Condition of this obligation is such that if Thos. Chedle and Frances his Wife do
truely observe all the agreements made between the above bound Thomas Chedle and
Frances his Wife and Joseph Hardee in a Deed of saile that then this obligation to be
void or else to remaine
In presence of JOHN OWEN 1719   Thos. Chedle
     DAVID D GEORGE, JANE X HARDEE   Frances ʃ Chedle
  At a Court held for Middlesex County the first day of March 1719
This bond was acknowledged and admitted to record

p.   KNOW ALL MEN by these presents that we JOHN HARDEE, MATTHEW HUNT and
505   WILLIAM GARDNER of Middx. County are bound unto our Sovereign Lord George
     in sum of ten thousand pounds of Tobo: this fifth day of Aprill 1720
   The Condition of this obligation is such that Whereas John Hardee hath obtained a Lycence to keep an ORDINARY at his House Now if sd John Hardee doth provide good and
cleanly lodgeing and dyett for travellers and stableage provender and fodder or pasturage as the seasons require for their horses dureing term of one year from the 5th of
April and not permit any unlawfull gameing nor on the Sabath suffer any to tipple
more then is necessary that then this obligation to be void otherwise to remain
Test   ZACH. LEWIS,   John Hardee
     WIL. STANARD   Matth: Hunt   Wm. Gardiner
  At a Court held for Middlesex County the 5th day of April 1720
This bond was acknowledged & is admitted to record

pp.   KNOW ALL MEN by these presents that we WILLIAM WOOD and JOHN MAYO of
505-   Middlesex County are bound unto our Sovereign Lord George in the sum of ten
506   thousand pounds of Tobo: this 5 day of April 1720.
       The Condition of this obligation is such that whereas William Wood hath ob-
tained a Lycence to keep and ORDINARY at URBANNA If therefore said William Wood do
provide good cleanly lodgeing & dyett for travellors and stableage provender and
fodder or pasturage as the seasons require for their horses dureing the term of one
year from the 5th day of April and not permit any unlawfull gameing nor on Sabbath
day suffer any to tipple more then necessary that then this obligation to be void otherwise to remain
In presence of us CHURCHILL JONES,   William Wood
        THOS. EDWARDS   John Mayo
   At a Court held for Middlesex County the 5th day of April 1720
This bond was acknowledged and it was admitted to record

pp.   THIS INDENTURE made the fourth and fifth day of April 1720 Between JOHN
506-   SMITH of County of Middlesex of one part and JOHN GRIMES of same Witnesseth
509   that for sum of seventy eight pounds of lawfull mony of Great Brittain he the sd
       John Smith sold unto John Grimes in his actuall possession by virtue of an In-
denture of sale for one year and by virtue of Statute for transferring uses into possession all that tract of land containing three hundred acres in County of Middlesex
whereon John Smith is seized in fee simple by Will Discent & conveiances from JOHN
NEEDLES deceased to whom a Patent was granted for Five hundred and fifty acres of
land which includes the sd Three hundred acres the sd Patent dated the twentieth day of
December 1667 which is bounded begining at a Pine on a point in the forke of a creek
and running West by North to a red oak by a path thence East to the ancient line of Mr.
ARMISTEADs land thence South East to a red oake known by the name of Sr. HENRY
CHICHELEYs Corner tree near the head of the sd creeke thence down the creeke to the
place it began
In presence of THOS. EDWARDS,   John Smith
        JAMES MILLER, JACOB CAWTHORN
   At a Court held for Middlesex County the 5th day of April 1720
John Smith came into Court and acknowledged his lease and release to John Grymes
Esqr and it is admitted to record ANNE SMITH also appeared and acknowledged her re-
linquishmt. of dower in sd land and it is admitted to record.
   KNOW ALL MEN by these presents that I John Smith am bound unto John Grymes in
sum of one hundred fifty six pounds of lawfull mony of great Britain this fifth day of
April 1720.
   The Condition of this obligation is such that if John Smith shall at all times keep the
agreements mentioned in Indentures without fraud that then this obligation to be void
otherways to remain
In presence of THOS. EDWARDS,   John Smith
        JAMES MILLER, JACOB CAWTHORN
   At a Court held for Middlesex County the 5th day of April 1720
John Smith acknowledged his bond and it was admitted to record

p.   KNOW ALL MEN by these presents that wee RICHARD DANIEL, STEAKLEY TOWLES
510   & CHARLES COOPER of Middlesex County are bound unto our Sovereign Lord
       George in sum of ten thousand pounds of Tobacco this third day of May 1720
   The condition of this obligation is such that Whereas Richard Daniel hath obtained a
Lycence to keep an ORDINARY at the COURTHOUSE of above County Now if said Richard

Daniel doth constantly provide good cleanly lodgeing and dyett for travellors and stableage provender and fodder or pasturage as the seasons require for their horses dureing term of one year from the third day of May and not permitt any unlawfull gameing nor suffer any person on the Sabbath to tipple more then is necessary that then this obligation to be void otherways to remain in force

In presence of W. GOUGH   Richard Daniel

                              Stokly Towles   Charles ✕ Cooper

    At a Court held for Middlesex County the 3d day of May 1720
This bond was acknowledged & it is admitted to record

pp.   THIS INDENTURE made the Seventh day of June 1720 Between WILLIAM HILL &
510-   FRANCES his Wife of County of Middlesex of one part and HENRY GILPIN & MARY
512   his Wife of same County of other part Whereas JOHN NEEDLES Father of WILLIAM
         NEEDLES of sd County of Middx. deced being seized in one plantation & lands be-
longing whereon he dwelt as also a parcel of land joyning to same formerly called JOHN
HEWS's land lying near containing together One hundred and fifty acres of land and
being so seized did by his last Will and Testament dated the second day of May 1686 be-
queath the sd premises to sd William Needles and his heirs forever which sd William
Needles died without heirs so sd premises became lawfully vested by way of survivor-
ship in sd Frances Hill and one MARY HUTCHESON only Daughters of sd John Needles
which said Mary Hutcheson having lately by her Indrs. transferred her title to the said
Henry Gilpin and his heirs the sd William Hill and his Wife and sd Henry Gilpin and his
Wife are not seized in the sd land & they now being fully agreed that sd premises should
be equally divided and that a just partition thereof by consent may be made between
them so as each of them may have their own parts that perpetuall division shall be had
in manner following that is to say that sd William Hill & his Wife shall have as their
part all that tenemt. formerly called by name of JOHN HEWS's land near the Shel Neck
in the lower part of the sd County and Henry Gilpin and his Wife shall have all that
Tenemt. where John Needles dwelt lying near Peanketanke River side ajoyning to the
part hereby allotted to sd Wm. Hill and his Wife

In presence of THOS. EDWARDS   Wm. Hill 𝒲
         HENRY ✚ FAULKNER   Frances Hill
                                                    Henry Gilpin
                                                    Mary Gilpin

    At a Court held for Middlesex County the 7th day of June 1720
William Hill and Frances his Wife & Henry Gilpin and Mary his Wife came into Court &
acknowledged ye within Deed to be their severall acts & deeds (the said Frances Hill
being first privately examined) which is admitted to record.

                              Test   W. STANARD   Clk

Finis W. S. Clk.

CHURCHILL. Armistead 72, 73, 74, 75, 88;
Elizabeth 4?, 76, 96; Madm. 40, 4?, 65;
William 3, 5, 18, 4?, 87, 96.

CLARKE. Edward 13, 15, 2?, 28, 3?, 61, 62;
John 3, 4, 11, 18, 36, 50; Robert 30;
Sarah 30.

CLAY. George 6.

CLERK OF COURT. Buckner 20; Dale 39, 96;
Epes 19; Hickman 3?, 62; Stanard 3?, 61;
Tayloe 29, 39.

COCKE. Elizabeth 15; Maurice 30, 43;
Mill of 43; Walter 12; William 61, 62.

COLE. James 80.

CONNER. Anne 14.

CONWAY. Edwin 19, 35.

COOKE. Thomas 61, ?5.

COOPER. Charles 10, 44, 45, 75, 93, 9?, 98;
Mary 10.

CORBIN. Colo. 35, 87; G. 3?;
Gawin 5, 11, 12, 31, 43.

CORDWELL (CARDWELL). Branch of 28;
William 94.

COUCH. Edwd. ?1, 94.

COUNTIES: Charles City 19; Essex 10, 19, 20,
30, 3?, 43, 49, 60, 75, 91, 93; Gloucester 3, 14,
65, 76, ??, 85; King & Queen 11, 15, 19;
Lancaster 10, 19, 29, 38, 87, 96; Northumberland 34; Princess Anne 20, 32, 33, 35, 44;
Richmond 86; Surrey 12; Westmoreland 33.

COX. Matthew 10, 11, 31.

CRANK. Elizabeth 89; Matthew 4, 79, 89;
Thomas 59, 86; Thomas Junr. 59.

CRANOVATE. Docter 4?.

CREEKS. Barbeque 59; Blands 83; Bonners ?3;
Morgains 87; Muddy 76, 91; Parrotts 76;
Robinson Mill 87; Sandy Point 91;
Sunderland 48, 89, 90; Wadeing Muddy 55.

CUFFELY. Mary 44.

CUMMINS. Angelo 21.

CURLIS. Thomas 54.

CURROTUCK. Albemarle 32, 33.

CURTIS. Adam 40, 63; Avorillah 41; James
Junr. 53, 86; John 2, 3, 12, 17, 18, 2?, 28, 31,
32, 33, 34, 36, 39, 40, 41, 45, 48, 49, 51, 54,
55, 56, 60, 64, 66, 69, 79, 83, 85, 86, 92;
John Junr. 34; John Senr. 34; Rice 1, 3, 36,
39, 70.

DAGLE. Patrick 29.

DAINGERFIELD. William 19.

DALE. Edmd. 39; Wm. 96.

DANALLY. Arthur 81.

DANIELSON. William 19.

DANIELL. Richard 4, 30, 69, 79, 83, 91, 92, 9?,
98; Robert 11, 12, 31, 36, 54, 89, 93; Robert
Junr. 12; William 4, 31, 3?, 41, 42.

DANLO. William 44.

DARE. William 2.

DAVIS. Benjamin 23, 24, 25, 26, 2?;
Elizabeth 68, 69; John 45, 46, 68, 94;
Mary 41; Thomas 65; William 62, 75, 80, 81,
83, 86, 8?.

DAWKINS. William 19.

DEAKER. William 47.

DEGGE. John 47, 63.

DIGGS. Auditor 2.

DOCKER. Edward 40, 60.

DODSON. Francis 64.

DOWNING. William 21; William Junr. 21;
William Senr. 21.

DUDLEY. Elizabeth 45, 46, 7?, 85, 94; James 13,
64; John 29, 45; John Junr. 85; John Senr. 85;
Mary 13; Richard 94; Robert 31, 32, 33, 35,
41, 44, 55, ??, 85, 89, 93, 94; Thomas 29, 41,
44; ??, 83, 84; William 13, 53.

EDWARDS. Richard 14, 76; Thomas 82, 86, 88,
89, 90, 91, 96, 9?, 98.

ELLIOTT. Elizabeth 31; 89; Thomas 13, 29, 32,
33, 53; William 29, 44, 77.

ENGLAND: Bound for 33; London 5, 18;
Middlesex 19; Westminster 18.

EPES. Littlebury 19.

EVANS. William 54.

FALKNER. William 3, 98.

FARGUSON. Allen 36.

FERNE. John 13, 61.

FIELD. Tho: 81.

FORRENS. Robert 5.

FOSTER. Elizabeth 44; John 21, 44.

FOWLES. Nicholas 40, 60;

FREEMAN. Henry 42.

FURNETT. William 64.

FURRELL. Anne 30; John 30.

GABRIEL. Richard 1.

GALLBREATH. Robert 86, 8?.

GARDNER. Martha 92; Ringing 5?; Thomas 4?;
William 14, 18, 22, 23, 35, 39, 44, 49, 50, 60,
6?, 79, 96.

GARWOOD. William 93.

GENERAL ASSEMBLY: Fee charged 9,10;
Leavies 14, 15; Precept for Holding Court 17,
18; Regulation of Grievances 58, 59; Storehouse
for Viewing Tobacco 52; Writt of Habeas
Corpus 8, 9.
GEORGE. Anne 82; David 20, 31, 84, 95;
Robert 38, 82, 83; Robert Junr. 82.
GIBBS. John 35, 54, 61, 92; Mary 47.
GILPIN. Henry 91, 95, 98; Mary 98.
GOARE. Jos. 61; Joseph 84, 85, 94;
Lucretia 85.
GODIN. Anne 47, 48; Thomas 35, 47, 48.
GOODLOE. Henry 1, 28, 36, 73, 74.
GOODRICH. Henry 13; John 94; Mary 94.
GOODWIN. Mary 55.
GORDON. Bridgett Charlton 22; William 1,
2, 6, 7, 8, 22, 64, 65, 66, 84, 87.
GOSS. Elizabeth 84; George 84.
GOUGH. W. 60, 66, 69, 71, 79, 98.
GRASON. Frances 29.
GRAVES. Alexander 10, 27, 31, 32, 37, 54;
Benjamin 19, 20, 87; Mary 28, 29.
GRAY. William 32, 83, 84, 86, 87.
GRYMES. Cha: 34; Charles 57; John 27, 47,
48, 57, 61, 62, 65, 66, 78, 84, 85, 94, 97.
GUTREY. Jane 93; John 60, 93.
GUTTRICH. John 81; Mary 81.

HACKET. Thomas 15, 66, 67, 78, 90.
HACKNEY. Allice 72, 75; James 32, 33, 51;
Joaner 75; William 64, 69, 72, 73, 74, 75,
77, 88.
HAINES. Charles 90; Margarett 90.
HAMERTON. Edmund 5, 6, 10, 11, 12, 31, 35,
57, 70.
HAMMETT. William 61.
HARDEE. Averilla 3; J: 11, 32; Jane 95;
John 28, 31, 44, 62, 81; Jos: 49;
Joseph 50, 54, 76, 79, 80, 84, 95.
HARDIN. George 59, 95.
HASLEWOOD. Thomas 13, 14.
HAWKINS. Nicholas 94.
HAYES. Henry 31; Thomas 76.
HEDGCOCK. Thomas 37.
HENEMAN. Thomas 12, 23, 34, 44.
HERRING. Anna 40; Jonathan 40, 47.
HEWES. Rebecca 40.
HICKEY. Charles 48; Elizabeth 28;
John 28, 29, 48.
HICKMAN. Henry 19, 20; R. 32, 33, 38, 61, 62,
63, 64, 69, 75, 78; Richard 37, 62, 64; (contd)

HICKMAN (contd). Thomas Junr. 11, 19.
HIDE. Jonath. 72, 73, 74, 75, 76, 80.
HILL. Francis (Needles) 91, 98; Frans. 92;
Leo: 37; Thomas 35; William 91, 95, 98.
HILLIARD. Martha 14, 89; Matthew 88, 92;
Thomas 92.
HIPKINGS. James 62, 72; John 2, 21, 44.
HODGSKINSON. Richd. 19.
HOOPER. George 30.
HORD. John 37.
HOSKINS. Bartho: 5.
HOUL. Elizabeth 31.
HUBBART. Thomas 94.
HUGHS (Hew). John 54, 95, 98.
HUNT. Amey 54; John 93;
Matthew 53, 54, 66, 69, 73, 90, 96.
HUTCHESON. Mary (Needles) 91, 98.
HUTCHINSON. Joseph 3, 5; Mary 3.

INDIANS: Mattepony Path 38.

JADWIN. John 30.
JAMAICA. Island of 86.
JAMES CITTY. Gen. Assembly 1680. 58.
JOHNSON. John 27, 40, 53, 63, 64, 65, 95;
John (Schoolmaster) 40; Jonathon 27, 37, 62,
63; Ralph 33, 35; Richd. 39; William 91.
JOLLEY. Dudley 23, 26, 61, 89.
JONES. Churchill 47, 97; Emanuel 96;
Henry 37; Humphrey 20, 42, 86, 87; John 11;
Mary 29; Rice 10, 11, 31, 37, 43; Roger 29,
47, 89, 92; Susanna 47; William 1, 11, 15, 21,
29, 30.

KEIGHLEY. John 4.
KELLY. Benjamin 65.
KEMP. Eleanor 49; Elizabeth 83; Matthew 1, 2,
3, 10, 12, 13, 14, 15, 22, 24, 28, 33, 34, 38, 39,
41, 42, 44, 48, 53, 54, 70, 71, 72, 73, 76, 80, 81,
83, 84, 85, 88, 89, 90, 96; Mr. 31; Richard 2.
KENT. Bayley 96.
KIBLE. Line of 46.
KIDD. Alice 67, 93; Thomas 28, 40, 54, 66, 67,
68, 71, 75, 90, 93, 94; Thomas Junr. 93, 94;
William 34.
KILBEE. Christopher 32, 88; Kathi: 88;
Land of 73; William 32, 88.
KILPIN. William 4, 15, 22, 34, 46, 57.
KITCHINS. John 30.
KNIGHT. John 87.

PAFFAT. Richard 25.

PAGE. Mann 76, 96.

PATE. Elizabeth 83; James 83.

PATEMAN. Lettice 53; Thomas 53.

PATHS: Curtis 39; Downing 21;
Mattapony 38; Old 10; Rowling 10, 37;
Town 38.

PENDERGRASS. Edward 30, 48; Elizabeth 30.

PERROTT. Pen: 12, 27; Penelope 76;
Richard 20, 27, 50, 56, 76, 78; Richard
Senr. 78; Robt. 44, 56; Sarah 50; Widow 50.

PERRY. Matthew 21, 37, 53, 57, 59.

PIERCE. Edward 54.

PINNELL. Jon 80.

PITT. Samuel 19.

POTTER. Cuthbert 4, 18, 38, 39.

PRATT. J. 96; John 5.

PRESNALL. Jacob 11.

PRESSENTER (PRESSON). Jacob 12, 28, 42.

PRICE. John 27, 30, 31, 48, 54, 56, 65, 66,
80, 85, 86, 88; Robert 95.

PRISON: Wortham to 23.

PRITCHARD. Uncle 25.

PRITCHETT. Roger 93.

PROVERT. Hannah 1; William 1.

PYNES. John 87.

RAY. Gabriell 62.

READE. John 77, 78, 88.

REIGON. John 93.

RENOLS. Line of 84.

RHODES (ROADS). Anne 72, 73; Elizabeth 72,
73; Hezekiah 72, 73, 77; John 68, 72, 73, 77.

RICE. Daniel 94.

RISK(E). Anne 73; James 22, 34, 73.

RIVERS: Peyanketanck 85, 98; Potomack 12;
Rappahannock 4, 12, 22, 65, 76; Yorke 5.

ROADES. Ezekiah 75; Hezekiah 71;
John 71, 75; William 75.

ROADS: Ferry 33, 35; Maine 4, 62, 64, 66,
67; Negro 66; The 89.

ROAN. William 27.

ROBERTSON. Wil. 10.

ROBINSON. Christopher 6, 7, 8, 22, 23, 24, 25,
26, 27, 32, 33, 41, 51, 52, 55, 60, 61, 64, 65,
66, 67, 77, 78, 79; John 4, 6, 7, 8, 23, 24, 25,
26, 27, 33, 34, 41, 52, 60, 63, 64, 65, 66, 70,
81, 82, 86; Mill of 89; Susana 43; Thomas 44.

ROSE. Elizabeth 60.

ROY. James 94.

RUN: Dragon Swamp 53.

RYAN. Edmund 64.

SANDIFORD. Frances 65, 88; Francis 40;
John 5, 50, 55; William 40, 55, 59, 62, 65, 88.

SCARBROUGH. John 85; Mackrory 65;
William 65.

SEARS. Mary 35.

SEGAR. John 27, 39, 45, 56, 57, 73, 74, 79;
Mr. 37; Oliver 16, 17, 22, 24, 27, 30, 31, 35,
36, 50, 65, 66, 68, 70, 76, 83, 84, 87;
William 62, 64.

SHELFORD. Richard 5.

SHELTON. Mary 14; Thomas 14.

SHEPHERDS. Ground of 40.

SHERIFF: By 6; Kemp 14, 15; Perry 59;
Seger 16, 17, 24, 27, 31, 37; Vivion 34, 45,
52, 92; Walker 74, 82, 83, 85, 86;
Wortham 56, 60, 61.

SKIPWITH. William 15, 33, 73.

SMITH. Alexander 4, 38, 39; Anne 97;
Augustine 77, 85; Edward 83; Elizabeth 4, 62
James 4; John 1, 2, 4, 6, 7, 8, 13, 14, 27, 32,
34, 36, 38, 39, 50, 51, 55, 57, 59, 61, 70, 91, 95,
97; Nicholas 86; Samuel 5, 39; Thomas 34,
48, 56, 60, 92, 93.

SOUTHARD. John 86.

SOVEREIGN: King George 52, 53, 57, 60, 61, 65,
71, 75, 83, 90, 91, 96, 97; Queene Anne 2, 5, 8,
14, 17, 18, 22, 27, 33, 36, 37, 43, 46, 52, 85.

SOWELL. Elizabeth 35.

SPOTSWOOD. Alexander 9, 18, 45, 52, 56, 59, 61,
74, 82, 83, 92.

STAMPER. John 16; Mary 20; Powell 20.

STANARD. William 1, 2, 3, 5, 13, 14, 15, 17, 18,
19, 20, 21, 22, 23, 27, 28, 30, 31, 32, 33, 34, 35,
36, 37, 38, 39, 40, 41, 42, 45, 46, 48, 49, 51, 52,
53, 55, 56, 57, 59, 61, 62, 64, 74, 75, 76, 81, 85,
88, 91, 92, 96, 98.

STANTON. Theophilus 5.

STAPLETON. Dr. 28; George 18, 31, 32, 54;
John 5; Thomas 5, 6, 31, 54.

STEEL. Thomas 16, 66.

STEEVENS. Anne 40; Christopher 87;
Richard 5, 40, 41, 53, 54, 57, 59, 63, 64, 65, 88;
Sarah 57.

STEVENSON. James 15.

STIFFE. Jacob 15, 26, 27, 28, 32, 47, 61;
Thomas 15.

SUMERS. Elizabeth 29; John 29.

SURVEYOR. Beverley 4, 75; Cooke 61, 75.

SUTTON. Chr. 59.